THE MANUAL OF BEAN CURD BOXING

TAI CHI AND THE NOBLE ART OF LEAVING THINGS UNDONE

PAUL READ

The Manual of Bean Curd Boxing:
Tai Chi and the Noble Art of Leaving Things Undone
ISBN: 9781836029069
Perfect Bound

First published 2010
2024 Edition by bookvault Publishing, Peterborough, United Kingdom
An environmentally friendly book printed and bound in England, powered by
printondemand-worldwide

CONTENTS

ALSO BY THE AUTHOR

The Tai Chi Illustrated Workbook:

Complete the workbook to discover which elements of Tai Chi most attract you and how best to learn them in this visual guide backed up with online examples in every chapter.

The Beginners Guide to the Tai Chi Form:

A simple 10 Step Tai Chi form that anyone can learn in a few weeks using this easy step-by-step method - all backed up with a free online course showing details of all the steps and moves.

This is Tai Chi: 50 Essential Questions and Answers:

The classic Q&A introduction to Tai Chi for those with a gentle curiosity.

One Last Thing: A Time Travellers Guide to the History of Martial Arts Philosophy:

The surreal time-traveling series of interviews by International Reporter Gerald Greene: featuring Lao Tzu, Kwai Chang Caine, Mr. Sanders, Alan Watts, Carl Jung, Dr Dolittle and all the greatest Tai Chi "influencers" from history.

All books can be ordered from https://taichi-store.com

COMMENTARIES ON BEAN CURD BOXING

If you never own another Tai Chi book, please own this one. Its irreverent look at Tai Chi... will make you laugh, it will make you think.

— WILL BROWN: THE TAI CHI PLAYER

There's a surfeit of wisdom and original exercises included that makes this a genuine classic of the genre.

— MARK ELLIS: CRAFT OF COMBAT

It is a great contribution to the world of Tai Chi.

— **BOB KLEIN: AUTHOR OF MOVEMENTS OF MAGIC**

Of the many books on Tai Chi I have read over the years, I can't remember being inspired by any of them as much as The Manual of the Bean Curd Boxing. This should be a 'must-read' for anyone.

— **BARRY CLINTON:** TAI CHI INSTRUCTOR

It's been a while since I wanted to read through a book twice but this one I'm going through again.

— GOOGLE REVIEW

What do Tarzan, gazpacho, gently-fried fish, and walking like a cat have in common? They are all part of Paul Read's unique, creative, and entertaining approach to revealing the heart of Tai Chi... This book is not a carbon copy or cut and paste of the writings of others. Its originality is what makes it refreshing.

— **BUCK BARNES: TAI CHI INSTRUCTOR**

I would recommend this book to any serious Tai Chi player as a 21st-century insight into the mysteries of the Tai Chi Classics.

— **MICHELE GIBSON** TAI CHI INSTRUCTOR

Explains the essence of Tai Chi without dwelling on form. A very useful addition, even to a seasoned practitioner... provoking, profound and with practical exercises that can be put into daily life.

— — JIM GRIGG

I dig the hell out of this book. This is probably one of the most entertaining and accessible books you could ask for on a subject that, in other hands, becomes just plain goofy in its earnestness.

— RICK RAAB-FABER

Irreverent, inventive, and funny. He does a good job of bringing Tai Chi and martial arts philosophy down to ground.

— ASONÍN D'ASTURIES

With over twenty years experience in Tai Chi my learning continues. Paul Read's gentle insights...add to the knowledge of wherever your practice has bought you to date. A great read.

— ANDREW JOHN WESTGATE

Introduction to the New Edition

TO THE 5TH EDITION

 If we can know anything with certainty, it is that everything we know is unquestionably uncertain.

WHY "THE MANUAL OF BEAN CURD BOXING"?

You may be wondering, why anyone would name a book "The Manual of Bean Curd Boxing"? Well, it's simple: Tai Chi, much like bean curd (or tofu, for the uninitiated), is deceptively soft yet profoundly resilient. Just as bean curd bends and adapts without breaking, the practice of Tai Chi teaches us to embrace flexibility and softness as the ultimate strength. Bean curd absorbs flavours, changes colour, adapts to the requirements of the recipe. In short, it is a substance that knows how to flow with life's challenges rather than forcing its way through them.

But there's more. "Bean Curd Boxing" isn't just a playful name; it's a philosophy. The Chinese writer, Lin Yutang, in his book *The Importance of Living,* argued that by constantly striving for completion or perfection, life inevitably becomes overcomplicated. Not everything needs to be finished, he  wrote, and that often, the most meaningful experiences in life happen when we allow ourselves to step back and let things be.

The first Bean Curd Boxing sessions were initiated by the teapot-mOnk in the early 1990s. These sessions embraced a hands-off approach, allowing each student to discover their own path at their own pace. Traditional teaching methods focused on memorisation and drills were set aside, as they often hindered true understanding. Students needed little more than a gentle nudge, a whisper in the ear, or a realignment of breath to adhere to the principles. After that, all that was required was to step back and let the rest unfold naturally.

WHY THIS EDITION, AND WHY NOW?

This latest edition of "The Manual of Bean Curd Boxing" comes at a time when the world needs it most. We're living in an era where everyone is constantly on the go, chasing one goal after another, and burning out faster than ever before. The pandemic, technological overload, and the relentless bombardment of news and social media have left many of us feeling overwhelmed and disconnected from ourselves.

That's why this 5th edition is more than just a reprint; it's a timely reminder of the wisdom Tai Chi offers in navigating the chaos of today's world. This edition includes new features designed to deepen your understanding and engagement with the material. Additionally, you'll find a new series of woodcut-style images of the main characters of the book: Ninja cats, Flamingos, Tarzan, Cheetah, Tortoises and Tigers. These illustrations are not just decorative; they're meant to provoke thought, stir the imagination, and bring the concepts to life in a way that words alone sometimes can't.

Plus, as a bonus, this edition adds a new chapter called the **Bean Curd Playground** in which you will find links to videos demonstrating the workshops that appear throughout the manual.

UNDONE

So, as you flip through these pages, remember: the greatest battles are often won not by fighting, but by learning the art of not fighting at all. Welcome to the gentle, yet profound world of Bean Curd Boxing—just in time for when we all need it most.

A NOBLE ART:

DOING LESS TO ACHIEVE MORE

In Tai Chi, as in life, the less you push, the smoother the flow. Leave it undone; perfection is overrated.

The underlying message of the digital age suggests that we can achieve more by doing less, an enticing proposition in a world where efficiency is often equated with success. This mantra, however, rarely transcends the surface level of modern sales pitches, espoused by new-age entrepreneurs and self-styled gurus who inundate us with an endless stream of information yet offer a conspicuous lack of true wisdom. The promise of "Less is More" has been co-opted, becoming a hollow slogan divorced from its deeper roots in ancient philosophy—particularly the rich, contemplative tradition of Taoism and the profoundly low-tech practice of Tai Chi Chuan.

In our fast-paced Western culture, we often find it challenging to comprehend the language of these ancient arts. Accustomed as we are to a world that prizes speed and efficiency, we struggle to appreciate the slow, deliberate pace of Tai Chi and the concise yet profound wisdom of Taoist teachings. To genuinely understand the concept of Doing Less, we must cultivate a new kind of literacy —one that not only teaches us how to Get Things Done but also embraces the noble art of Leaving Things Undone. This is about learning to step aside, to get out of our own way, so that life can unfold naturally, in accordance with its own rhythms and flows.

Enter Bean Curd Boxing, a practice that speaks this new language —a language that redefines traditional concepts of strength, grace, and softness. By invoking the presence of our animal friends and teachers, Bean Curd Boxing encourages us to reconnect with these elemental qualities. Yet, as with any philosophy or practice, words alone are insufficient to inspire real change. That's why the Manual of Bean Curd Boxing is not merely a text but a guidebook for transformation. It includes ten workshops, each designed to gently explore and implement the philosophy of Bean Curd Boxing in a way that promotes genuine, lasting change.

ABOUT THIS MANUAL

The first nine chapters of The Manual of Bean Curd Boxing delve into the core ideas that traditionally drive our actions: our pursuit of happiness, balance, simplicity, and health. These are universal desires, yet our approach to fulfilling them is often misguided, leading us to tie ourselves into knots—both physically and mentally. The manual begins by showing us how to untangle these knots, starting with the correction of bad posture that restricts the power of our breath, and moving on to address the patterns of our most recurrent thoughts and behaviours that keep us stuck in unhealthy cycles.

In Chapters 10 and 11, the focus shifts from introspection to action, taking the principles explored in the earlier chapters out into the world. These chapters show us how to integrate the soft yet firm exercises of Bean Curd Boxing into our daily routines, helping us to increase our energy levels, strengthen our constitution, and adjust our pace of life to a more sustainable, healthier rhythm. This integration is not just about physical movement; it's about harmonising our inner and outer worlds, allowing us to move through life with greater ease and purpose.

The final chapters of the manual provide a contextual history of the arts that make up Bean Curd Boxing. Understanding the origins and evolution of these practices gives us a deeper appreciation for the wisdom they contain. As the saying goes, the best advice on how to move forward often comes from looking back, and these chapters offer a rich tapestry of insights that inform our present journey.

BENEFITS OF PRACTICE

While this manual does not promise enlightenment, it offers something equally valuable: practical advice on how to keep moving. Movement, as it turns out, is the essence of life. This movement is not confined to physical actions but extends to the subtle rhythms of our breath, the pace of our stride, and even the softness of our gaze. It is reflected in the flow of air and water, the paths of the planets, and the invisible currents of the digital world. By learning to move with intention, we discover the art of progressing by doing less, of arriving on time by slowing down.

And when the time comes to Get Things Done, especially when those around you are caught up in a frenzy of activity, you will learn to take a step back—perhaps to go and make some tea instead. This simple act of stepping away from the chaos often leads to unexpected solutions to our most pressing problems. If this approach seems contradictory, that's because Bean Curd Boxers delight in the interplay of opposites.

Throughout the manual, you will be encouraged to engage with this Noble Art through a sense of **play** rather than study. Studying is far too serious an approach for a Bean Curd Boxer for it carries with it the weight of accomplishment, the pursuit of an end and all the pressures associated along the way. Playing, as we do with an instrument,  allows ideas to flow and the exercises enable you to experiment without the pressure of immediate judgment. These are important steps in the process of letting go and embracing change.

In keeping with this playful spirit, most chapters conclude with a section called *Ask the Teapot*. This Question and Answer session addresses the most common queries that beginners may have as they embark on their training. It serves as a reminder that in Bean Curd Boxing, there are no fixed ideas; everything is in a state of flux, and even the most well-argued points may be best contradicted at some later time. This openness to contradiction is not a weakness but a strength, reflecting the dynamic, ever-evolving nature of the practice.

ASK THE TEAPOT:

Q: What exactly is Bean Curd Boxing?

A: It is the reclaiming of soft posture, soft breathing, and soft thinking to give us back more energy, more rest, and yet still achieve all that needs doing.

Q: Soft thinking? Is that why it is called Bean Curd?

A: Many people mistakenly believe that there is but one sort of Bean Curd. But Bean Curd comes in many shapes and forms: Silken Bean Curd has the consistency of custard and is therefore far too soft for what we need. Stinky, meanwhile, is just, well, too stinky, and the 1000 Layered, despite its Taoist-sounding name, is just a frozen variety and as such is far too cold for what we have planned. Instead, as Bean Curd Boxers, we will concentrate on the Firm Variety, for when pressed it yields and then pushes back, demonstrating an adaptability essential in a world that changes so quickly and so often. Bean Curd Boxing (the 'Firm Variety') draws on the soft principles of Tai Chi Chuan and applies them to a world that is increasingly digitalised, fractured, and segregated; Bean Curd Boxing shows us the path to find balance.

Q: Do you have to practice Taoism, Meditation, or Tai Chi Chuan to learn Bean Curd Boxing?

A: Certainly not. Neither do you need to chant, buy any beads, or map any Ley Lines. This manual is an excellent starting point for any of the above practices, but it is more than just a manual. The aim of this book is to try and bring the ideas alive, to go beyond the definition of words and beyond the arguments about principle. The aim is, very simply, to provide us with the basic tools to turn life upside down and inside out, leaving you forever changed and forever open to change.

Q: What does the Art of Leaving Things Undone say about Shoelaces?

A: It is often said that you can't learn something new without first letting go of something old. It's the same with your shoelaces. When your shoelaces are badly knotted, do you carry on tying them into more knots or do you stop for a moment and say: hey, why don't I try undoing them first?

UNTYING THE KNOTS:
YOUR FIRST STEP AS A BEAN CURD BOXER

 What relief in untying a tight belt, a shoelace, a hair tie, a neck tie or a knot of tension in your stomach.

At the core of Bean Curd Boxing is Tai Chi: a relatively old discipline that offers us a different language for interpreting this manic world in which we live, and for exploring alternatives that complement rather than confront these permanent cycles of change. The language of Tai Chi is not based on words, but rather on movement and silence - finding alignment and patterns of energy that follow us as we breathe and move through this world of transience and insubstantiality. It has been said that we have two ears and one mouth, and that we should learn to use them proportionately. So in Tai Chi we communicate less with the mouth and more with movement, breath and touch - actions that employ all our listening senses, so that we can read a situation from the slightest contact with another human being, whether it be an accidental brush against someone in a crowded bar or a sensual caress in a candle-lit bedroom.

By observing how someone responds, how someone breathes or how they shift their body weight in response to our touch we can learn this new language of consciousness.

To learn something new as a Bean Curd Boxer, however, it is always advisable to discard something first. Thus this chapter of this manual attempts to do just that by showing us how to let go - or untie the knot - of those things that stand in our path:

1. Unhappiness
2. Imbalance
3. Complexity
4. Ill-health.

I. UNTYING THE KNOT: UNHAPPINESS

The economic and political crisis that spread during the early part of the 21st Century provoked a global outcry, not just to reform the system but to replace it with something more meaningful. At last people everywhere were asking if life could promise more than just servitude, endless consumption and the dissatisfaction that always accompanies this lifestyle. But if satisfaction is not to be found in the activity that consumes most of our conscious life on this planet, then where can it be found? Perhaps it could be purchased online? Ordered from a shopping wish-list?

Alas, for most of us, our working lives leave us with a sense of emptiness and a deep underlying worry that the real meaning of life has somehow strolled past our front door and forgot to stop by. For some, this realisation comes as the first exciting job promotion quickly leaves us as unsatisfied as before. For others it is when the kids have left home or when, after so many years of yearning, retirement finally arrives and there is an unease and discomfort with such an abundance of space in our lives.

In search of meaning, we stumble out beyond the front door only to tumble from one global recession to another, one health epidemic to another, or yet one more violent conflict over dwindling global resources. As consumers, we are encouraged to ameliorate such conditions by snacking on products pretending to be food - but this lasts only for so long. At some point we have to sit down to eat a proper meal - a meal that will satisfy our soul's hunger for true expression and our stomachs' appetite for true tastes in the foods we buy. Our minds crave something too, a taste for honesty amongst politicians, economists, or news outlets, and curiosity to see how society might work if it didn't only revolve around personal acquisition and consumption.

All research into the causes of such deep dissatisfaction points to the need to live more consciously: to understand that what we feel inside does not depend on what happens to us, but rather on our attitude towards and our interpretation of each and every experience. In other words, to look deeply at the things we do and take our sense of value and meaning from ourselves rather than simply our job descriptions, our postal codes or the manufacturer of the cars in our garages. We are either wealthy or destitute according to what we are, not according to what we have.

In order to be able to focus in this way, a higher level of internal energy is needed: an energy that is not dissipated by the nonsense of life, but instead reinforced and reinvigorated by simple activities and simple pleasures that we enthusiastically choose to follow. The answer is universally the same: Change your daily routine.

- Drink more water
- Breathe deep and often.
- Sleep well - even if just a few hours.
- Practise regularly some form of exercise.
- Find a moment in every day to be silent and do absolutely nothing.

These are the fundamentals of living a more simple and deeply satisfying life. Yet, simple sentences do little to explain how we move from where we are, to where we would like to be. Words by themselves can inspire, but rarely can they show us the way forward. To go beyond the text, and to discover the action, another language will be necessary.

2. UNTYING THE KNOT: IMBALANCE

As a Londoner who once lived near the financial quarter of the city, I would peddle though the busy streets each day on my way to work, dodging the lines of pin-stripe suits, cutting across the angry traffic lights on red, and illegally speeding up one-way streets to ensure I would arrive on time.

Returning, the journey would be a little less frantic, but I still found myself mounting pavements to avoid stopping in congested areas, or weaving through oncoming traffic so as to maintain the illusion of purpose that is born from speed and haste. But then there would always come a moment when I  would have no choice but to stop at one of the busiest junctions in the city. With adrenaline pumping through my body, I would sit in the middle of the street astride my push-bike, with my left arm protruding into the oncoming traffic as double-decker buses, taxis and motorcyclists sped past mere inches from my fragile frame. My breath would be shallow and high in the chest, eyes flickering in all directions, and fingers tapping out impatient rhythms on the edges of the chrome handlebars. At this moment the illusion of safety in movement disappeared, replaced by a world in chaos visible only in stillness. Finally, when a clearing eventually appeared, I would dart between the clouds of carbon monoxide and enter a quiet and hidden alley behind the empty warehouses of the city perimeter. Behind me, gradually fading into the distance I left the roar of engines, the screech of hastily applied brakes and the anger of car-horns. Immersed in another world, I would free-wheel gently along, slowly awakening to the new sounds of the barrow-boys wheeling out their evening market stalls, the Indian restaurants sending out olfactory tapas and the regular skimming sound of brake-blocks wearing down as they rubbed the rims of my warped back wheel.

Twenty years later, although I now live in southern Europe, I often still feel as though I'm perched in the middle of that highway with an endless queue of speeding traffic demanding my attention. These days the road I navigate is a digital one, and the traffic zeros and ones, but the journey is fundamentally as unsustainable as that suicidal London bike ride for one reason alone: there is no balance.

Without balance (or a good set of stabilisers), we soon fall off our bikes. Balance is important. Without balance we cannot see the pace at which we work; everything looks blurred. Look out the window of a high-speed train, and the detail is lost. Try to focus on the environment as you speed along the motorway and the objects of interest pass you by before you have had the chance to engage.

How does this thirst for speed affect our health, our relationships, our work and our sense of who we are when we enter the slip road and we can no longer maintain a speed of over 100kph? How do we function once more at a calmer and healthier pace when everything

appears unbearably and tortuously slow? To cultivate greater balance, we must learn to go slower. We must learn to take the side roads more often and leave to others the addictive pace of the motorway.

Some have argued that speed and haste have their place. Doing several things at the same time, for example, is a new skill in the digital world, a skill that the current technologies enable. But there is a Russian proverb that says, *'If you chase two rabbits, you will not catch either one.'* Multi-tasking is a little like rabbit catching; it is the great illusion of productivity, the fantasy that we can accomplish more and more at digital speeds by splitting our attention into ever-smaller parcels of activity.

However, we only need to look at the laws banning the use of mobiles whilst driving to see how completely incapable we are of placing our attention meaningfully in two places at once. We may think we accomplish more, but in truth, we do the opposite. If you have one important task to accomplish, you can choose to devote all your attention (about 120 bits of information) to the single task, or you can split it up, dilute it and distribute it over several tasks. Either way it's the same 120 bits, and one thing gets done well, or half a dozen gets done poorly.

Tai Chi reflects this rule by teaching us the benefits of undivided attention and the accomplishment of the single task by bringing our breath, mind and physical body together. This fusion of activity may appear contradictory, but it is not about doing several disconnected things at once: rather it is about eliminating those habits that prevent the body, mind and breath from naturally working as one. The Bean Curd Boxer therefore chooses to let things take place and align him or herself to the movement. A contemporary example is that of the Slow Movements: Slow Food and Slow Travel are all part of a global shift that has emerged over the last few decades in response to a world that encourages pace at the expense of value.

If we learn to slow down, we begin to see beyond the haze of activity, beyond the dust cloud rising from the hooves of the pack-animals ahead that run and run in circles. By breathing deeply and by stopping activity, we become aware of the passage of the moon, the flight of the carpenter bee, the wind ruffling a palm leaf, or the synchronised stretch and yawn of a sleepy dog. By slowing down we may hear the sigh of a loved one, and who knows, maybe even think a little about why we do the things we do.

3. UNTYING THE KNOT: COMPLEXITY

There is a danger that comes with too much of any one thing, data included. If information overload is threatening to disconnect you forever from the world of texture and wind, or if you find yourself increasingly impatient with the pace of life and unsatisfied with the prospect of silence, then perhaps it is time to let go of some of the baggage and tread more lightly on this fragile Earth. However many social media messages, text messages, or status updates you receive, information consumption can never amount to simple wisdom, for it is only through the pursuit of stillness and observation that such fruit is acquired.

For many people, wisdom is a worthy sacrifice for mobile internet access and a faster connection speed, where access to information has come to be an end unto itself. But beware, as information is not neutral. It carries with it promises of insight and understanding, education and enlightenment, and it seduces by previewing a world it can never deliver. Unless we can filter the offers of more and more, we will drown in a sea of less and less, unable to differentiate the meaningful from the meaningless.

In learning, therefore, Bean Curd Boxing prioritises patterns instead of words and employs the body as well as the mind. There is an emphasis on the undoing rather than the doing in order to avoid clutter and to fully live in the moment. For what was the reason for acquiring so much if by so doing we are inhibited from fully engaging with our time on this earth?

One day there will be a power cut, AI virus, or an internet failure and our access will be blocked. One day the antennae will fall down and the smartphone will revert to a flat camera. On that tragic day will come the realisation that the rest of the planet still marches merrily on and that instead of observing it from the other side of a screen, we could be participating — or better still — constructing that world.

Perhaps, after the initial shock is over, we will be distracted by the wind catching a branch overhead, the shadow of a cat passing by, or a shaft of sunlight that has illuminated a few particles of dust dancing in the corner of the room. Then, maybe conscious of the movement of time and the absolute richness of the moment, we will see the futility of chasing paper tigers.

4. UNTYING THE KNOT: ILL HEALTH

The collected arts of the Bean Curd Boxer aim to bring back consciousness to our movements. As we have seen, consciousness comes in many forms, by slowing down, learning a new language and unplugging ourselves now and again in order to notice a whole lot more about life. But we also need to pay more attention to our health. The quality of our daily lives is too often shaped by nameless aches and pains, joint stiffness, a loss of flexibility, breathing difficulties, balance problems, concentration and relaxation issues, and the general susceptibility to whatever is 'going around'. The list is seemingly endless as we yearly succumb to conditions that affect our physical makeup and mental perspective. Paradoxically, for many of us, our health deteriorates despite eating 'better', taking regular exercise, and each week getting fitter.

In the confusing search for better health, we are only conscious that something is missing, something hidden behind all the paraphernalia of the fitness and diet industries, something beyond the reach of the Pilates DVD, the home gym, or the all-meat diet – – and that is to simply do less.

The big question is how? How do we do less and yet not only get more done, but get more done with less effort and less time? How do we transform the ideas of simplicity, slowness, and conscious living from the words of a book to the actions of our lives? The answer lies in the practical applications and energy awareness exercises outlined in this manual on Bean Curd Boxing: letting go of old habits, tension, ideas, and inhibitions. To live healthier and to live fuller is not about enrolling on a course or subscribing to a plan of action, it is simply about doing less. Once you have completed the training of the Bean Curd Boxer, you will step out onto the street with less weight, carrying less baggage but with a stronger constitution and a softer glare.

ASK THE TEAPOT:

Q: "Slow down", "simple wisdom", "do less": It all sounds so easy, yet we know that life is much more complicated than a new-age slogan.

A: This wisdom is far more ancient than the latest trends in meditation or what your local evening classes program may offer this year. The advice in this manual comes from the collective writings of the Bean Curd Boxers that go back to distant times and cultures. This advice has surfaced again now, precisely at the moment when society is experiencing a giddying pace of life and is tempted to just keep striding forward without first looking back.

Q: Should I then give up my Smartphone and my AI assistant?

A: That is your decision. Technology can liberate as well as intoxicate. Used with focus and awareness, mobile devices can be timesaving, excellent organisers for collecting the nonsense of life and depositing it all in a digital folder to be brought to your attention only when it is really necessary. This, in turn, can leave your mind clutter-free to concentrate on more important issues.

Q: Should I get a digital 'to-do' list?

A: Well, you could try something analogue such as Bullet Journaling, but whatever your choice of tools, ensure it can get your thoughts out of your head. Set up a recurring delete of all your to-do nonsense once a week and see how liberating it is to have a constantly clear to-do list. Productivity may well drop, but that is a small price to pay for clarity and a blank page.

Q: Sometimes I see the words written as Tàijíquán, T'ai-chi-ch'üan, T'ai-chi, Taiji or Tai Chi. What are the differences between them all?

A: Spelling.

Q: And the difference between Tai Chi and Bean Curd Boxing?

A: Bean Curd Boxing is the everyday application of Tai Chi and other related disciplines to the world outside the classroom. It is a compilation of ancient and contemporary wisdom bundled with practical advice about posture, breathing, and attitude. You may see it also called 21st Century Tai Chi and its starting point is: If it works for you then use it - If it just sounds silly, then leave it where it is and move on.

Although this book draws heavily on the lessons of Tai Chi and the wisdom of Taoism, it is not in itself a book on either of these two disciplines. If you were looking to learn Taoism, you would be better advised to find a Sage.

Sages generally do not advertise their services, so they may prove difficult to track down. Gurus however are a different species altogether and in these days of social media hype, are multiplying like the plague and should be approached with a healthy dose of scepticism and a big stick.

If you are just looking to learn Tai Chi, then the simplest and most direct method is to find a local class. If this isn't possible, look for an online course (preferably one that embodies laughter, informality and a big dose of undoing things). It is not recommended to learn all the Tai Chi moves from a book alone, as they will require the support and back-up of a local class or online references. The intricate posture changes, breathing patterns, ideas and applications make a place of learning, either local or digital, essential. However, Bean Curd Boxing does not focus solely on the methods and practices of Tai Chi. Bean Curd Boxing is best learned by observing yourself and the things you do each day. It is learned by eliminating the unnecessary, and by developing the skills found in this manual so that they slowly integrate into your daily life patterns.

Q: What about learning with my VR headset?

A: This will certainly be novel and entertaining and in time, prove to be a useful tool in your learning toolbox. But, in the meantime, try and find a class nearby, or a course online. New directions have been taken with online tools that now introduce novel teaching methods and content that traditional classes cannot provide. Time and location are factors too - sometimes it's not always possible to find the class you need at the times you are free and close to the place you live. This is why more people today look for supplementary tools - videos, books and online courses. Check out the back pages of this book for more info.

CHAPTER 3

FROM STILLNESS TO MOTION:
STANDING UP FOR OURSELVES

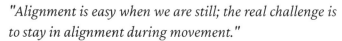

"Alignment is easy when we are still; the real challenge is to stay in alignment during movement."

I t is not enough to only know how to put one foot in front of another, or how to mount a kerb in order to safely cross a road. We still need to know how to spot an oncoming bus. Likewise, wellness is not just a question of practising the right exercises; it is also the ability to recognise when something is coming straight for you and to adjust accordingly. A well body can avoid the onset of muscle tightness, cramps, stiffness, tension, and joint aches because it recognises the approach of ill-health. The secret is in learning good posture. Not the ludicrous posture rules we were taught at school such as 'sit up straight', 'don't slouch', and 'chin-up' that made us tight, tense, and inflexible. Instead, we need to adopt the posture that comes from natural movements so that physical tasks become less arduous and mental tasks less daunting.

POSTURE AND MEMORY

Good posture starts with observing the cycles of our behaviour, taking note of the small and the overlooked, and paying close attention to the roots of misalignment. When our body is tired or dysfunctional, it rarely has the reserves to embrace the changes necessary. So we must start with an awareness of misalignment, for what follows is a release of tension as muscles that are not in use relax, and breathing deepens as the chest softens and sinks. Ligaments and joints take over from over-used muscle groups and ultimately a new way of movement is unveiled.

We have already seen that to acquire something new, we must first let go of something old, and so it is with posture. Our first priority is to learn to let go of the bad habits that keep the muscles in tension and keep the body out of balance. In a class of Tai Chi, a teacher may adjust the angle of an elbow to loosen a tight shoulder, or the tilt of a chin to relieve neck ache and improve balance. These small changes are made repeatedly in class until they integrate into all our movements and Tai Chi becomes a living part of us. Outside of a class, we will need to run down the checklist mentioned later in this chapter. However, remember that letting go of old habits is far more difficult than taking on new ones. Letting go requires a realignment of not just bones, muscles, and body weight, but a fundamental change in outlook, perspective, and attitude.

LETTING GO OF MEMORIES

Sometimes the problem lies in our history. At some distant point in the past, a muscle constricted to prevent an injury, or tightened in expectation of a blow and consequently, the memory becomes held in the muscle fibres to be replayed whenever the body anticipates the return of an old behavioural pattern. The problem is that the body remembers too well. It interprets new circumstances incorrectly and thinks that the same outcome is likely, so sends the muscle into spasm for self-protection.

To counter such memories, we need to re-educate our muscles and offer an alternative response to the stagnant memory reflex. Muscles learn from habits and therefore can be taught to readjust to changing circumstances. The following exercise — a simple preparatory stance from Tai Chi — can be employed anywhere and at any time. Like all good Tai Chi exercises that adapt well to Bean Curd Boxing, there is beauty and effectiveness in the exercise: it can be embraced into your daily activities every time you stand still for just one moment. It just takes a few seconds to run down the list and suddenly you are retraining your body, so that energy will flow once more, stagnant pain will disperse, and change will once more be a real option.

Unlike other power-training schedules, Bean Curd Boxing only practises Soft Stances. These are postures that put the body at ease, allow deeper breathing and muscle relaxation, yet leave the body agile, fluid and prepared for either movement or stillness: whatever the moment requires.

THE FOUR STAGES OF GOOD POSTURE

One advantage of integrating Bean Curd Boxing into your life is the knowledge that no one other than you will know you are practising. The four stages of good posture awareness should be practised everywhere: at the bus stop, the railway platform, the pedestrian crossing, or when consulting that text message you just received. Take each stage slowly: learning and practising one session before moving on to the next.

I. FEET

Your feet should be shoulder width apart and touching the floor with the same sense of connectivity as your palms would have if they were in contact with the same surface. This means you can feel your weight being supported between the heel and the ball of the foot. Try rocking gently forward and back, and then from side to side to increase your awareness of weight distribution on the soles of your feet. Do you notice when your weight is more on the heel? Do you notice when your weight is more towards the instep? Now stand as you would normally and feel in which part of your foot the weight falls. Can you sense that? Now try and bring the weight to the centre of the foot. Practise this weight awareness exercise until it becomes second nature, then move on to 'Knees'.

2. KNEES

Following on from stage 1, slightly unlock your knees so that the large muscles of the legs take the bulk of your upper-body weight. By opening the joints a little you free the pelvis so that it can be tucked under (as in a pelvic tilt), thereby releasing lower back strain and re-aligning the spine. Avoid locking any of your joints.

I once had a job as a walking sand-wich board advertiser, ambling along the Strand in London. Disad-vantages to this line of work included friends pointing at you from the other side of the street and laughing and shouting: "That'll teach you to major in philosophy". The benefits, however, are that you  have to entirely rethink your posture. When the boards are strapped tightly to your torso, the combined pressure from the boards against your chest and backside result in pushing your pelvis under and aligning it with your lower back. This is the posture you should imagine adopting in Tai Chi.

3. THE UPPER BODY

Your hands and fingers should be relaxed until their natural curve is allowed to return. When we let go of holding on, our body follows a natural curve. Drop your shoulders; keep your elbows low and your chest relaxed to allow for deeper breaths. As a general rule, do not hold yourself up; rather, let everything respond to gravity. Releasing these muscle groups allows your body to relax and dissipate built up tension. With a relaxed upper body, it is possible to engage in deeper breathing, and with deeper breathing your body becomes lighter, more agile and capable of adapting to changes in circumstances.

4. THE HEAD

Your neck should be elongated, and the head lifted from the shoulders as if suspended from the ceiling. Imagine you are a giraffe. This helps balance, improves circulation, and again helps with that sense of lightness when in movement. Finally, your tongue is held lightly in contact with the roof of your mouth, just behind your upper front teeth. This is the basic aligned physical posture, both in stillness and in movement and should be employed every day.

ALIGNMENT AND ROOTS

Connecting with the ground and learning to use it for support, balance, and strength is called 'Rooting' and is the next step in learning good posture. In the previous exercise, we focused on the soles of the feet and looked to see where the weight was distributed. This was our introduction to 'rooting'. Another way to develop a root is by opening up the joints and relaxing tight muscles so that the full body weight drops to the ground instead of being held in the neck, shoulders, chest, lower back, waist, and knees.

Rooting, therefore, is about lowering your centre of gravity and bringing your awareness out of your head and down into your body. In this way, it is not just your skeletal structure that supports you, but the ground too. It does this by absorbing the body weight that you have learned to release from your joints and muscles. When that force is needed again, it is drawn back up the legs, directed by the waist, and released through the arms like water rushing through a floppy garden hose

For a very visual image of someone rooting, take a look at the old black and white videos on YouTube of Cheng Man-Ching pushing away students who run towards him. From where does this strength derive? Watch again, slowing down the film and you will see how his legs are like springs, absorbing and then releasing body weight as he uses the ground to first yield to and then repel the student. This, despite appearances, is no superhuman feat; just a fine example of rooting, combined with relaxation, better breathing, and a superb sense of timing. And of course, a body that can remain in alignment during movement.

ALIGNMENT AND MOVEMENT

Alignment is easy when we are still; the real challenge is to stay in alignment during movement. It is only in movement that we are given the opportunity to observe how our body responds to a thousand subtle factors, from gravity and muscle memory to balance and breath. It is therefore in movement that we learn the lessons of good alignment. So how do we practise incorporating these small changes to our body in a class of Tai Chi? We do so by practising what is known as the Form. The Form offers us an opportunity to watch energy transforming itself, gradually evolving, expanding, and contracting as each posture emerges out of one and into another. It is like the movement of the waves or the two elements of yin and yang in play and thus deserves a chapter on its own: Form - The Methods of Movement and the Mother of All Patterns.

ASK THE TEAPOT:

Q: What shoes should I wear when rocking forward and back on my feet?

A: Avoid hiking boots, diving boots, football boots, or skis. Other than that, the choice is yours. Remember, uniforms and special training clothes only accustom your body to perform when wearing these clothes. Bean Curd Boxing, if it is to be usable at all, is best employed when least expected, without having to rush to the nearest phone booth and change into your superhero clothing.

Q: When I tilt my pelvis and try to move, I feel like I'm watching an episode of Monty Python's Ministry of Silly Walks.

A: Keep going. This is a good sign.

Q: I watched that Cheng Man-ch'ing video, and it looks to me like his students were somewhat compliant. Wouldn't you say?

A: Perhaps. Compliancy in demonstrations is common, partly because students are trained over years and years to venerate their teachers, especially in public. So, demonstrations often exaggerate a "master's" abilities, concealing what may be ineffective routines. This is not to say that all demonstrations are fixed, but it is good to be aware of these tendencies.

THE DANCE OF PATTERNS:

TAI CHI FORMS AND INFORMATION OVERLOAD

 The essence of Tai Chi resides in the movement of your breath and the flow of energy through your body.

B ean Curd Boxing is a language of patterns, and the mother of all patterns is found in the Tai Chi Form. The popular image of Tai Chi is that of a seamless slow-motion dance performed by vast groups of elderly individuals shifting back and forth in unison in the morning mists of a public park in China. The Form is both the first contact many people have with Tai Chi and, at the same time, the ultimate expression, for within its moving timeline are all the elements of the art: breathing, alignment, posture, and even history.

THE MOTHER OF ALL PATTERNS

The sequence of postures in the Form is like the words of a story: Look at the words by themselves, and they have little meaning, but combined and placed in order, they can say something of great beauty and significance. Like all languages, it is not just the choice of words that is important, but how they relate to each other that gives meaning to the whole phrase. So in Tai Chi, we study not just the postures themselves, but how these postures flow from one to another, and how each is defined by its predecessor and successor.

At times, there appears to be repetition, but the body's alignments are redrawn like constellations in the night sky, and although from one angle things may appear the same, from another an altogether new perspective is reached. This becomes another challenge for all of us: how to maintain the rhythm and flow through one set of circumstances after another. There is nothing like the Form to truly test our posture as we learn to apply techniques against an ever-evolving and moving background.

Forms differ from one style to another: the Extended Form, the Short Form, Narrow or Wide, Straight or Curved. One school may accentuate lower postures and more extended joints, whilst another will stress a higher posture and more contracted movements with curved and smaller openings. But all variations are just accents in the language of Tai Chi, expressing no more than a difference of emphasis. No style is better or worse than another. There is only you.

A QUESTION OF ACCENT

Not that long ago in Spain, anything other than a clean Castilian accent was frowned upon and considered inferior to the purity of speech from the centre of the country. Then, in the early 1980s, a new President was voted into power in this fragile new democracy. Originating from Andalusia in the deep south, he brought to the government in Madrid a strong and undiluted Andalusian accent.

Gradually, the old opinions about the deficiencies of the Andalusian accent dissolved as people learned that difference does not necessarily mean better or worse and that in the expression of difference we find all the wonder and awe of the world.

In the world of Tai Chi, we are still awaiting the arrival of a speaker from the outer territories, and in such an vacuum, debates rage as to the correctness of one accent over another. History, however, shows us another story in which the Form has adapted and evolved over time, reflecting the people and the place where it is taught. The dance of energy and the pulse of life that is the Tai Chi Form cannot be stilled nor set in time.

WHERE ARE THE PICTURES OF THE TAI CHI MOVES?

With such a diversity of styles and techniques in the world of Tai Chi, there is little point in presenting instructions here for each of the moves, even though most new students—and many older ones too—avidly seek certainty in their postures. Books vary, classes vary, and so too do instructors of the same styles. The advice of a Bean Curd Boxer is that confidence and surety in the Form come not from studying the geometrical preciseness of each move in a book, but rather from learning how to combine the various postures with the breath, a good sense of balance and coordination, and a relaxed state of mind. It is not the fine details that are important, but the principles upon which they are based.

THE SEARCH FOR SPACE: PARKINSON'S LAW

There is a second reason why no instructional images of Tai Chi postures are included here, and that is due to Parkinson's Law, i.e. that information expands to fill the space available. In order to contrast with our overfilled lives, space is often a sought-after element in a Tai Chi class. Unfortunately, during more meditative moments, teachers have a tendency to fill the available space with numerical, geometrical, or anecdotal information. Once again, the threat of data overload invades the lives of those who are actively seeking less, and this time it strikes at the heart of the class. Instructional information, i.e., the conveying of angles, measurements, percentages, body weight, the interpretation of names, postures, and descriptions, all conspire to overload the new student with excess data.

Bean Curd Boxing is about the unlearning of the old and the finding of space in our cluttered existence. The rest is just reference material that can be easily acquired through any number of books or articles available on the Internet. (There is a full range of published manuals by recognised teachers that do this job thoroughly, detailing body parts, breathing directions, the angles of the feet, the distribution of weight, and even accurate compass directions for those who seek this type of knowledge.) For these reasons, the Bean Curd Boxer emphasises the patterns, the shapes, and the feel of the movements, and allows the details to come later.

Al Chung-liang Huang, in his inspiring book "Embrace Tiger Return to Mountain," attempted to convey this essence, offering classes that appeared alive, organic, and interactive. While Alan Watts, his friend and contemporary, spoke of life as fundamentally a pattern of immense complexity. Watts said that what we call our "self" or "identity" is simply a constant pattern, like the flame of a candle, a momentary manifestation of energy in a recognisable shape.

Al Chung-liang Huang used this idea of patterns to promote an overall flavour of the moves rather than detailed directions. The same approach is valid whenever there is a vast amount of information to take on board. Too much information then disables rather than enables.

So how can you employ these ideas in your practice? When learning a sequence of moves, try to concentrate on the swings and circles of movement and on the waves and pulses of energy moving through your body. Follow these movements and the movement of your breath, and you will find that the essence of Tai Chi resides there, and not in the precise angle of your ankle or your eyebrow.

ASK THE TEAPOT:

Q: If I shouldn't be thinking of angles and other details, what should I be focusing on when practising the Form?

A: There is an interesting poem on Tai Chi written by Alan Ginsberg in 1984 called "In My Kitchen in New York" that addresses this question. Whilst the poet is practising his Form at home, he tries to concentrate on his technique. However, as he moves from one posture to another, he finds his mind flickering from the unused apron hanging on a wall, or an unpaid electricity bill.

As a beginner to the Form, these mind games will happen often. Simply let them go. Try not to think about the moves; instead, go back to feeling the Form. Enjoy playing with the moves and the unique way they blend and fuse with one another. Explore the tactile experience of moving consciously through the air, focusing on the flow and the motion, without worrying about precision. If you are learning a sequence in a class, simply copy others and don't worry about memorising or knowing everything. There will be plenty of time later to learn the order of the moves and where everything ought to be. By then, you will have hopefully recognised the futility of using your mind to remember such details.

When you feel more confident with the general order of moves, you can then focus on weight distribution, muscle relaxation, regulating breathing, and finding the circles in the movements. All these elements take time to learn, apply, and internalise. Don't feel tempted to rush into them. Tai Chi is something to gradually work at over the course of your life.

Q: And after I have learned all of that?

A: Then you will find yourself back where you started: performing without thinking, playing without trying, moving without effort. Just doing. It will be how it was at the beginning, only somehow different.

Q: I don't have as good a sense of balance as others in my class and my co-ordination is awful. It is going to take me much longer to learn. Will I hold up the class?

A: Try not to fall into the trap of comparing yourself with others. Some students are good with choreography and learn patterns quickly. Others have better memory, deeper root, spatial awareness, balance, suppleness, grounding, and so on. Each student has his or her strengths and weaknesses. What is important is that we don't make comparisons as this activity benefits no one. As everyone starts the learning process at a different pace, some will move faster or slower in various directions. Despite our different learning methods, we all end up at more or less the same spot, at more or less the same time.

Q: I understand what you are saying, but I'd still like some precise instructions about angles and positions. At least some photos!

A: Have patience. Learning Tai Chi is not like downloading an app. It's a process and a commitment. If you really need to know the moves today, take a look at my book, The Beginner's Guide to the Tai Chi Form that uses images, descriptions, and online examples to walk you through all you need to know.

Q: I know the postures quite well now, but still feel I lack flow. What should I do?

A: Don't get hung up on the postures. Ultimately, the transitions between them are the really important parts. Look for the birth pangs of the next posture within the death throes of the existing one.

Q: I bought one of those books with angles and weight shifts. There just seems so much detail. How can you ever learn all of this information?

A: First, throw away the book. Try not to focus too much on individual moves. Give up the effort of following every detail. Become silent inside: listen and watch other people with your deeper self. When you are calm, complex events appear simple. When you are calm and your breathing is slow, you smile much more at the world.

Q: I'm not attending a Tai Chi class. I'm just learning Bean Curd Boxing with this book. What can I learn from this section?

A: All the exercises in this manual are similar to learning the Form. Perhaps you will start with postural work, focusing on just lower back and knees. Then later you will add softness to your chest and shoulders and become more conscious of your breath. The names may vary from book to book, school to school, but the principles are the same.

Q: I have heard it said that Bean Curd Boxers breathe through their feet. Can breathing be a part of the Slow Movements too?

A: Now that we have looked at posture, it is time to turn our attention to breathing, for when we combine breathing with posture, we get not only interesting health benefits but also interesting chapter titles.

FROM TARZAN TO TAI CHI:
REDEFINING STRENGTH THROUGH BREATH

 Breathing: it's like tea — when done right, it warms the soul. When done wrong, it's just hot water.

In the last chapter, we examined posture by learning to align different parts of our bodies. In this chapter, we will apply the concept of alignment to our breath. By focusing on our breath, we can more easily concentrate on specific parts of the body, including our feet, as we will see later.

Breath awareness uses the vocabulary of Bean Curd Boxing: rhythms and patterns. By recognising, adopting, and following rhythms that occur both inside and outside ourselves, we can learn to attune our efforts with the natural course of events. There is no mysticism here, nor is any jargon intended when we refer to an awareness of breath. It's simply a way of saying, look for the patterns our bodies want to use, the rhythms they naturally want to follow. This is not difficult since they are constantly vying for our attention, dancing at our side wherever we are. We just need to learn to see them.

BREATHING IS NO SHALLOW ACTIVITY

We can live without food for weeks, perhaps months. We can live without water for hours, perhaps days. But without breathing, we cannot survive for more than a few minutes. Breath is our most direct means of engagement with life. Our participation in this ongoing mutual exchange is truly miraculous. It is elemental, perpetual, and so delicately balanced that our breath can help sustain a planet. When we breathe, we interact with everything that lives, has ever lived, and will live. Breathing is no shallow activity.

Learning to breathe deeply and fully, alongside good posture, can bring subtle but significant changes to our health: the body relaxes, and in relaxation, our different parts begin to work better and together. The mind and the body start moving to the same rhythm, slowing down and finding a more compatible pace of life.

HOW THE EXERCISES WORK

In learning the Tai Chi Form, we are often distracted from the real point of the exercise by trying to remember what we are meant to be doing. But, with the breathing exercises, the simple repetitions allow us to concentrate on the feeling of the moves, the rhythms, the coordination of muscle and bone, and the circulation of the breath.

Although following such slow repetitions will allow the mind to wander now and then, this is okay.

We just need to be conscious of such wandering and gently bring our attention back to the rhythms and patterns.

On a purely physical level, the gentleness of the exercises works the joints and ligaments, helps reduce their stiffness, and improves our sense of balance, posture, and coordination.

On another level, by constantly focusing on the simple and repetitive moves with coordinated breathing, we enter a simple meditative state that cuts out the stresses and strains of the day, allowing space, time, and energy to re-inhabit the body.

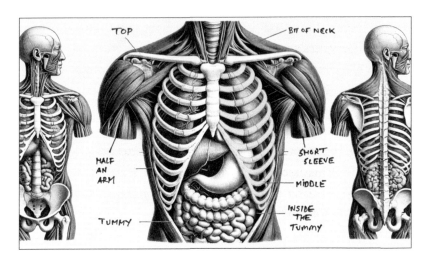

ANATOMICALLY SPEAKING

When we begin our practice in Tai Chi, we're often given words or phrases related to practices or parts of the body that leave us puzzled: 'Focus on taking your energy down to your Tantien,' or 'put your mind in your lower Tantien,' you might be told during a breathing meditation. These instructions are about as helpful as the anatomical chart here would be to a student of physiology or medicine.

Here, we shall explore the physiology of breathing related to the art of Bean Curd Boxing in a little detail, and although it may look like a dry and rather stale topic, the contribution from Tarzan and Cheetah will, I hope, bring more interest to the subject and its rather important lessons for those seeking the secret of Feet Breathing.

If we look at the lungs, we can see they are encased in a cage formed by the diaphragm below and the chest wall to the sides. When we breathe, we employ two separate groups of muscles to expand the rib cage: the diaphragm and the intercostal muscles. The diaphragm is a muscular sheath separating the chest from the stomach, a convex dome that contracts, flattens, and expands the space above it, thereby allowing air to be sucked into the lungs. The intercostal muscles are found between the ribs and are mainly responsible for the expansion of the chest. During normal relaxed breathing, the stomach gently moves up and down as we breathe in and out. This is due to the diaphragm pressing down during inspiration, causing the stomach to bulge outwards. A newborn child breathes this way, but as the child gets older, the breathing pattern shifts from abdominal to intercostal, and during adult life, breathing is almost exclusively intercostal. This leads us into the age-old problem of Tarzan's Chest.

TARZAN'S CHEST

As adults, when we think of taking a deep breath, we subconsciously think of Tarzan: not so much about Cheetah or the invisible fastening of Tarzan's loin cloth - though that may, of course, be a personal preference - but rather the permanently  inhaled stomach and expanded upper chest that became such a trademark of the Earl of Greystoke.

Yet, paradoxically, this widely promoted chest position actually makes breathing much more difficult and keeps the body in a tense and rigid state. The truth is that Tarzan would never have made it as head of the Wild Beasts with a chest held in constant tension because he would never have been able to yodel and swing from vine to vine while sucking his stomach in at the same time. Off-camera, he would have had to slow down his breathing and use his diaphragm, belly, rib cage, and lower back. In other words, he would have had to use 'abdominal breathing', and this would have forever changed the posture - and probably the poster - of the Lord of the Jungle.

WORKSHOP 1: HOW TO BREATHE LIKE THE EARL OF GREYSTOKE (BAD EXAMPLE)

1. Attach a couple of vines (in an emergency, try using a couple of trouser belts) to an overhead curtain rail.
2. Inhale, suck in your stomach, and push out your upper chest.
3. Exhale, swinging at speed from one vine to another with a chimpanzee on either shoulder.
4. Just as the chimps are about to tumble off, start yodelling, inhaling, and perusing the floor for concealed elephant traps.

WORKSHOP 2: HOW TO BREATHE LIKE A BEAN CURD BOXER (GOOD EXAMPLE)

1. Try lying down with your hands on your abdomen and watch what happens as you breathe in and out.
2. Breathe through your nose.
3. The abdomen will expand on inhalation and sink on exhalation.
4. Slowly, your breathing will become deeper and slower.

WORKSHOP 3: HOW TO BREATH LIKE A BEAN CURD BOXER (EVEN BETTER EXAMPLE)

1. Sit on a chair with your back straight.
2. Breathe through your nose.
3. Place your right hand on your upper chest and your left hand on your abdomen.
4. As you inhale, your left hand should rise a little, and your right should remain still.
5. Exhale as much as you can while pulling your stomach in a little.
6. As you inhale again, note how your abdomen fills by itself.

CHEETAH'S CHATTER

Some of these exercises may feel awkward at first, and you may question the effort to relearn breathing while you are experiencing no problems with your current method. The prospect of a sculptured Tarzanesque chest may even still appeal to the more jungle-oriented among you, particularly those who have spent years in front of gymnasium mirrors defining those pectoral lines. However, try to switch the focus of your training towards health and energy and away from ripping apart muscle fibres. In time, your breath will become smoother, calming, and energising. In time, you will come to enjoy having a greater lung capacity, increased self-confidence, and a relaxed stride that this simple change in breathing can impart.

Remember, for all these exercises to work, it is important not to hold your breath but instead to keep it flowing and rhythmic. Bean Curd Boxing is not about holding a static pose, but rather about engaging in a pattern of movement. Tai Chi differs here from other exercise regimes in that the breath is generally not held in place. Instead, it flows continuously, in one uninterrupted cycle, like the gentle ripple of hanging vines beneath the African canopy.

Try these exercises at night before going to sleep. They may even help turn off the Cheetah Chatter in the treetops of your mind.

THE CONUNDRUM

If you have an overactive nighttime mind - known as monkey chatter in some circles - then your evening schedule is probably not yours at all. Perhaps you have just adopted someone else's pattern, and maybe what is needed is to search for your own. Either the hour of retirement is too early, or you need to wind down before going to bed. Some people try to stay as active as possible until they cannot stay awake any longer - watching TV, reading, or prolonging screen time. This, however, can encourage the mind to keep on chattering.

Others follow different patterns by preparing themselves for sleep with routines and exercises that involve stretching tight muscles, going through specific breathing exercises, or drinking vast quantities of herbal teas.

How do you find your own pattern? The answer is in the search. Do not wait for the solution to appear before beginning your search, for you may have a very long wait. A Bean Curd Boxer recognises that solutions are often found in the act of doing and rarely in the process of planning. Set off down that road. Start the journey, even if you are not sure where it will end or even which direction to take. All questions will be answered en route.

BEAN CURD BOXING WORKSHOP: BREATH WATCHING

When you are watching TV, listening to music, or perhaps when you next see an argument coming your way, try to remember to pay attention to your breath. Ask yourself: is the breath deep or shallow? Are you holding your breath when it may be better to let it out? Try to notice when this happens, and begin to watch what happens as other people's breath becomes shallower or deeper according to the circumstances.

As you practice this exercise, you will find yourself more and more conscious of your own breathing habits, and this awareness will help you to gradually shift from shallow breathing to abdominal breathing. The process always starts as a conscious exercise, but in time it will blend in and become part of your general approach to life.

ASK THE TEAPOT:

Q: So, these breathing exercises - these patterns and rhythms - will they help me concentrate better, improve my physical well-being, and allow me to relax? Will they help my coordination, nervous system, blood flow, joint movements, and slow down my thoughts so that I can think more clearly and with less stress?

A: Yes.

Q: But is any of this really necessary? I feel fine. Do we not live longer now, eat better, exercise more regularly, and are we not in generally better condition than ever before?

A: Do not be fooled by statistics. We are very much in worse shape physically than our ancestors. It is certainly true that we now live longer and have eliminated many contagious diseases, but this has mainly been due to improvements in public sanitation, health care, and housing. In terms of good body alignment, balanced muscle tone, and natural full breathing, we are in a truly appalling condition.

Q: Posture, movement, and breath, then are all it takes to be well?

A: Attention to those things will help a lot. But there is still something else that links them all together, in fact something that links everything that is, was, and will be. An essential ingredient to any Bean Curd dish: something known as Qi (pronounced Chi).

Q: Qi as in Cheetah?

A: No, Qi as in energy.

CHAPTER 6
FROM FEET TO SPIRIT:
WIND BATHING, FEET BREATHING, AND THE
GRUMBLINGS OF YOUR STOMACH

 What is Qi? Think of it as Wi-Fi. You can't see it, but when it's strong, everything flows.

I n Bean Curd Boxing, we talk a lot about this energy called Qi. It is a concept known as Ki in Japanese, Prana in Sanskrit, Mana in Polynesian, and Ruwach in Hebrew. But in English, there is no direct translation, so we usually refer to it as energy. However, when we refer to energy, we can mean many different, but not necessarily related, things: we could be perusing our electricity bill with horror as we read how many joules we have consumed or referring to the spirited, dynamic, and animated personality of our pet chimpanzee. Qi embraces both of these interpretations and a whole lot more, for it carries within its broad definition the weight of life itself.

FOLLOWING...

The concept of Qi has long been debated in both the East and the West. Volumes have been written, arguments waged, and still, there remains great uncertainty not only as to its benefits but to its mere existence. For the Bean Curd Boxer, such debates are academic, for we seek only those practices that enable life to proceed at a smoother pace, irrespective of scientific validation or spiritual verification. Instead of a definition composed of words, we look for an experience that arises from action.

...THE GRUMBLINGS OF YOUR STOMACH.

If you try the breathing exercises in this manual, you will experience the flow of Qi initially as a feeling of warmth or a tingling in the hands. In time, this develops into a more solid pulse or wave of energy that moves through the body. This experience is common to most practitioners, yet is difficult to verify objectively. It is also almost impossible to explain since it is energy and it is spirit; it is abstract and at the same time very concrete; it is nowhere and yet it is everywhere. Qi is the intricate and interwoven substance that embraces us physically, spiritually, and mentally. In other words, try to think in broader terms than just your electricity bill, for this is just one very small part of the whole picture. Remember what Bruce Lee said in the opening scenes of Enter The Dragon when his student concentrates on his master's fingertip pointing to the sky:

 "Don't concentrate on the finger or you will miss all the heavenly glory"

Or more colloquially - don't miss out on the donut by concentrating on just the hole.

To understand energy, we have to look beyond the electricity or gas bill, beyond the nutritional listings on a box of Dunkin' Donuts, and learn to see the world as a constant interplay of life-forces. We need to be able to distinguish the moon from all the fingertips pointing at it.

This still leaves us with a rather abstract definition of what we mean by Qi. In fact, the more evidence we seek for objective confirmation of Qi, the less likely we are ever to find it, because it cannot be understood with just the mind. It is an interesting dilemma and one that reminds me of a moment in The House at Pooh Corner when Rabbit is running back and forth trying his hardest to work out an exit from the forest, and in the process goes deeper and deeper into the woods. Meanwhile, Pooh merely follows the 'Grumblings of his Stomach' and walks straight home. Sometimes, a dependence on the mind alone cuts off our sensory capacities and diminishes the possibilities of exploring new paths. As someone far wiser than I once said: "If you want to know the taste of something new, spit out the chewing gum first."

QUANTUM PHYSICS - ANOTHER LANGUAGE

If subjective experience proves far too—let's say—subjective for you, then consider the case of the Vibratory Cell. Often, the first problem we encounter when thinking about energy is how to conceptualise it, so instead, we associate the thing itself with its expression: the windmill, the solar panel, the lump of coal, or the log of olive wood. But these are sources or collectors of energy, visible—and often static—manifestations. However, energy is never static; it is shifting about inside and outside your body. Everything is in flux, and everything is moving in relation to everything else.

Through the practice of focused breathing, we can learn to perceive that vibration, to reach out and connect with that constant shift and movement. This is the purpose of these exercises: to develop our sensory awareness of the subtle changes in the air around our bodies.

If all this sounds far-fetched, then consider a more contemporary explanation for Qi in the theory of quantum physics. Within every cell of our body, each molecule and atom is in a constant state of vibration. Taken all together, they produce enough energy to change the properties of the space that they occupy. This phenomenon occurs both inside and outside the body (a distinction that bears less weight for the Bean Curd Boxer), and so, with training in not just tactile, but general sensory development, an awareness of changing states can become conscious.

Fundamentally, it is a process defined by different vocabularies. For some people, one explanation has sense and meaning; for another, it is the use of a different vocabulary altogether. Rather than get hung up on trying to agree on the choice of words, we can learn to let go of owning a definition and leave each person to take the one that suits his or her purpose best. For the Bean Curd Boxer, any definition is limited without taking us beyond the words themselves. For definition to have value, it must focus on the body rather than just the mind, for it is there that we will find the circularity of breath and the underlying patterns that can ignite the movement of the Qi as it travels through the body.

How then do we develop such sensory awareness? The answer is to simply practice the exercises in this book every day. Additionally, you will need lots of fresh air, a tranquil place under the shade of a cherry tree in full blossom, and preferably one that looks out over the dawn mists of a quiet and undisturbed valley.

If, however, like the majority of people on this planet, you do not have daily access to such a view, select any space where you can feel the wind on your body, a ray of sunshine on your cheek, or just the chill of the morning air around your ears or fingertips. Any and all of these will help in focusing both your state of mind and the surrounding environment, for it is precisely this relationship that we are attempting to cultivate.

Avoid centrally heated or air-conditioned rooms. You are looking for a connection with the world outside that magnifies exposure and limits exclusion. You are looking for an engagement with life, a way to reawaken all your senses and leave behind the daily activities that disengage us from the 'Grumblings of our Stomachs'.

WIND-BATHING

Exposing the body to the elements of wind, sun, and water can be stimulating and invigorating as well as healthy. If you find yourself close to the coast and have the opportunity to swim at a nudist beach, seize the opportunity. If, after a swim, you are fortunate enough to find yourself on a pebbly beach, try Naked Multi-Tasking by walking up and down to dry yourself in the wind and to give your feet a massage at the same time.

Simple? Yes, these activities are simple and, in many cases, obvious, but they also help expose us to a life outside the walls of our houses and our safety zones. Exposure—and not just the naked kind—stimulates our synaptic growth: our nerves readjust to new conditions, and our senses literally adapt and grow according to new challenges and exposures. Once something as simple as wind-bathing causes this process to begin, our senses become more alert and ready to convert all moments, all circumstances, and all surroundings into opportunities to improve our health and deepen our connectivity to the world. In short, we begin our training in the art of doing without doing: Bean Curd Boxing.

Wind-bathing is not always convenient nor possible for everyone, so we must adapt our exercise to our environment and specific landscape. For indoor practice, the Breath Watching exercise in the previous chapter is an excellent start, as is the Posture Checklist for better alignment and the development of rooting. Or simply open window, and stand close by.

To maximise the quality of your home training, ensure you have plenty of natural light, some fresh air flowing in through an open window, space for your body and mind to move about in—and a good supply of Mother-in-Law's Tongues.

If not Mother-in-Law's Tongues, try to get Money Plants from friends or relatives, as people tend to over-cultivate them at home and consequently are always on the lookout for enthusiastic recipients. Both these plants are particularly good at absorbing carbon dioxide and producing oxygen. Have as many as you can in your house or workspace, and grow them tall, not only to cover that stain on the wall but to clear the air and the contents of your head.

Then, when everything is set up, you will be ready to combine all that we have looked at so far and begin the little-known practice of Feet Breathing.

FEET BREATHING

Feet Breathing is an ancient Bean Curd practice that promotes the idea of rooting, grounding, and breathing deeply in order to merge with the dust of the world. Many critics argue that the lungs are closer to the chest than the ankles, but this is a moot point. What we are concerned with is the sense of connection with our breath, our posture, and the earth on which we stand.

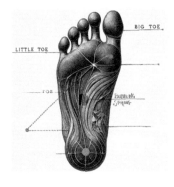

As a plant draws energy from its roots, so too can we draw support from the earth. It is the soles of our feet that create this link, which physically put us in touch with the ground and serve as our roots. By focusing on this point of contact, adopting a relaxed posture, and engaging with deep breathing, we can learn to ground ourselves wherever we are and whatever the circumstances.

WORKSHOP 4 : FEET BREATHING

- Maintain contact with the floor using the 3 Points of Balance. There is one point beneath the big toe, one beneath the little toe, and one in the middle of the heel.

Keep all three in equal contact with the floor whilst standing in the posture we learned earlier.

- Be aware of any tendency to move towards one point or another, moving from one side to another, or simply keeping more weight on one particular point.
- Now, imagine a point between the 3 points. This is referred to as the "bubbling spring" and forms the source of feet breathing energy.
- Unlock the joints and relax the muscles to allow the lungs to pull up the energy from the ground.
- Use your imagination to think of smoke, water, light, or the hole in a donut—it really doesn't matter—just imagine something traveling up through the three points, merging at the "Bubbling Spring" and then moving up into your chest.

Whatever you do, try not to allow distracting notions of what is anatomically possible to get in the way. Just because there is no clear pathway from the sole of the foot to the soul of the body in your anatomy book does not mean that the exercise lacks value. On the contrary, employing your mind to play with physical boundaries is what it is all about.

Feet Breathing is just one example of using your mind to visualise energy coming up from the earth and moving through the body, but it takes time for the mind and body to work in such a new and unified way. You have to practice and condition the body to receive stimuli through all of its senses, which is similar to learning a new language. To help, try taking off your shoes now and then. It is good to not only feel the ground beneath your feet, but to develop a sense of touch with the soles of the feet, in the same way that you may feel the surface of water with the palm of your hand. But do not confine yourself to that plush carpet or tiled hallway—walk out over the earth, the grass, and the sand on a beach. Better yet, do the unexpected and go out in the rain and dawdle in a puddle—for there is nothing that stimulates those synapses like the unexpected.

Attune yourself to the weather: If it is sunny outside, then go outside. If that is not possible, then open a window and focus on the warmth of the sun on the top of your head and the gentle caress of a breeze on your arms, and let that feeling, like the weight of your body, drop down to the soles of your feet. If it is cold, then take that sensation and let it move again through you. Don't try to hang onto any sensation, just note it and then let it move on.

To breathe, then, is to open ourselves to all things. Firstly, to recognise the patterns of energy that are present, then to be able to reach out and connect with them, and finally, to be able to take up what is on offer.

As I watch the eyes of my cat following some strange spirit force passing through the house, or when I listen to my dog interrupt its own snoring to wake up and growl at some visitor that is about to ring the doorbell, I become aware that my senses are indeed dull by comparison. In your practice of Bean Curd Boxing, try turning your mind into a magnifying glass and placing your attention on one sensation, one part of the body, or one small movement or pulse of Qi. Some students imagine themselves practising Bean Curd Boxing as if they were moving through water or Swimming On Dry Land. Forget for a moment your rational voice. Use your imagination whenever you can, employ it wherever you can, and watch the way the world changes shape. It is like smiling and frowning: The more we smile, the less we can physically frown. Try imagining how you wish your life to turn out, instead of rationalising it.

ASK THE TEAPOT:

Q. If I want to go straight home, I use Google Maps. Why would I follow the advice of a fictional animal?

A: Don't fall into the trap of dismissing good advice merely because it arrived via a cartoon bear. Stomach Grumbling, or if you prefer the latin name - borborygmus - reminds us that digital navigational aids can lead us up one-way roads or into rivers when divorced from intuition and pots of honey.

Q. Has 'Grounding' here anything to do with coffee beans?

A: Grounding means the ability to centre yourself by simply reconnecting to the earth—and in a sense—recharging your level of energy. Everything depends on staying relaxed, as worry, stress, and tension stop the flow. Calmness, softness, and imagination, on the other hand, all increase the charge.

Q. When you say: 'tension stops the flow', what do you mean?

A: Search YouTube for the classic fight sequence at the end of Way of the Dragon when Chuck Norris and Bruce Lee face each other under the arches of the Coliseum, and you will see an example of what happens when one person falls back on tension whilst another simply lets go. At the beginning, Lee suffers at the hands of Norris's more ritualised fighting style until he decides to break with all styles, to adopt no style, as Lee would have said. He flirts with a bit of boxing, a bit of this, and a bit of that, and in so doing exposes Norris's inability to move outside a rigid pattern. No matter how good we are at one thing, the moment someone steps outside our sphere or self-imposed boundary, things begin to fall apart. Watch what happens to Norris as this process begins: he becomes increasingly tenser and reliant on his structured responses even though they prove increasingly useless. Lee captured the essence of his philosophy by writing:

Not being tense but ready, not thinking yet not dreaming, not being set, but flexible—it is being wholly and quietly alive, aware and alert, ready for whatever may come.

Q. Why not quote Obi-Wan Kenobi from Star Wars while you are at it? He had something to say about the 'flow' too.

A: True, but Han Solo also said: "Hokey religions and ancient weapons are no substitute for a good blaster at your side," and I think that is as relevant today as it was then.

Q: Why should I want to learn to Breathe with my Feet when my mouth seems to be coping perfectly well?

A: Feet Breathing teaches your body to function as a complete unit —interrelated, interdependent, and interconnected with the earth. It forms part of the entangled foundation of Bean Curd Boxing and the general movement towards constructive change. Start with the basics of breath and interconnectivity, and you will develop a strong base, a forceful imagination, and enjoy a new pulse of energy.

Q: Should I sit or stand when thinking of the 3 points?

A: Either. Standing, though, has advantages as it can help identify weight points in the soles of the feet.

Q: Will being better-balanced help me?

A: Yes. Keep the knees slightly unlocked and stop the hips and waist tilting backwards by tucking your pelvis under a little. Attaining better physical balance enables you to adapt to external pressures and not lose your connection or your base. Add deeper breathing with the benefits of a tension-free body, and you have the basis for a simple but positive approach to life.

Q: But I don't feel any connection to the ground. In fact, I don't feel anything at all!

A: Try patience. Try imagination. Try removing the hiking boots.

Q: I've removed the boots. But there are other things in the way. I just keep thinking that it's physiologically impossible.

A Bean Curd Boxer does not reside solely in the material world. The really important stuff of life sits on the edge of our sensations and on the perimeter of our perceptions. Think about someone you love, who is no longer with you. What do you remember of their real essence? Their finger nails? Their shoes? Or their spirit?

When thinking of what the physical body can or cannot do, try not to think of Dr. House. Think of Dr. Seuss and let the imagination fly.

FINDING THE CURVE IN THE STRAIGHT:

TAI CHI'S RHYTHM OF TIME AND SPACE

 Straight lines get you there faster, but curves teach you the dance.

F eet Breathing can help us in grounding, which is built upon good posture and awareness of the breath. By applying these two principles to everything we do, we will begin to see the patterns we reproduce in work and play with ever-increasing clarity. Once we learn to see these patterns and the energy surrounding them, we can decide which are worth keeping and which should be discarded.

KEEPING AN EYE ON THE TIME

Spain is a country that has its own working timetable: The first shift starts at 10am and continues until 2pm, but even this is interrupted as bars fill with office workers for a collective round of coffee and toast between 10 - 10.30am. After lunch, workers return for a second shift from 5 or 6pm until about 8pm. This schedule allows for a leisurely 3-4 hour lunch break and a short siesta between shifts. The rest of Europe has consistently criticised Spain for not adopting the more universal 9am-5pm timetable. Brussels still occasionally shakes a bureaucratic finger, tutting and sighing at the anachronisms of the Iberians. However, Spain has firmly held onto its traditions, maintaining this pattern of work and play despite pressure to change.

Now, others are beginning to recognise the benefits of working this way. There are good reasons to live life at a different pace, but it requires changing our view of time. While we continue to see time as linear, we will continue to believe that if we do not use it, we will lose it. Time is money; therefore, if we idly watch it pass by, or—heaven forbid—sleep through portions of the day, we are missing out on earning more money and the opportunity to consume yet more consumables.

If we see time not as linear but circular, like an airport baggage collection belt, there is no rush to accomplish or consume, as all things will inevitably come around again.

Seeing life as an airport baggage collection belt has other benefits. It enables us to see repetition, the importance of curves, and the attraction of loops. Curves, for example, are more than just aesthetically pleasing to the eye: Think about an arch compared to a square doorway. Which tempts you to enter? Which tempts you to pause and run your fingers over its surface?

A peaceful walk along the canal with your dog or a stroll along a curved country lane encourages exploration and discovery; they promise a journey of slow awakening and stimulation. Motorways, on the other hand, offer little more than the option of moving into autonomous control or playing dangerously with the navigation display. The real problem with straight lines is that every time we come across an immovable object, we have to stop and change direction. Travelling along curves means that the flow will always be with us, as we learn to circumvent immovable objects by easily shifting body weight and thereby learning to yield.

Curves also bring us back to ourselves; they serve to remind us of our roots and the cyclical pattern of movement and breath. Inevitably, there are times when cycles, like the memories held within muscles, get caught in loops. To break out of such repetitive patterns, we need to search for a loophole in the slow, repetitive exercises of Qigong.

THE FLAVOUR OF FRUITS

Qigong exercises—or energy breathing exercises—offer wonderful opportunities to focus on patterns, curves, and loopholes. The simple repetitions of these exercises allow us to watch and observe our patterns over time, noting what comes up again and again. These sets of breathing exercises come in many shapes and sizes: the Eight Pieces of Gold, the Eight Embroideries, the Silk Exercises, or the Farmers Exercises, to name but a few. If your school, video, online course, or Sifu states that there is only one true set of Qigong exercises that will carry you along the path to Qigong Heaven, then bear in mind what others, far more knowledgeable than I, have said on the matter*:

 Each man belongs to a style which claims to possess truth to the exclusion of all other styles... Stylists... cling to

forms and go on entangling themselves further and further, finally putting themselves into an inextricable snare.

— BRUCE LEE

The rigid adherence to traditional forms in which practitioners focus more on maintaining the purity of their style rather than understanding the practicalities of the art are what Bruce Lee referred to as a "fancy mess." The essence of the arts is lost in favour of maintaining form and tradition

For most new students, the division and sub division of routines are of little importance. Whatever series of exercises you practice or however many exotic animals are evoked during your meditative breathing exercises, try to put aside such comparative labels and focus on the essence of the exercise. Embrace what you do completely, and try not to fall into the trap of comparing your style, the name of your founder's family village, or your teacher's recent lineage with that of another: Fruits come in more than just one flavour. When eating an apple, do not deny the existence of the humble banana.

In Bean Curd Boxing, we do not concentrate on a singular set of Qigong exercises. Instead, we focus on exploring the fundamentals of Qi so that you will be able to apply those skills to any exercises and patterns that you encounter in life.

WORKSHOP 5: SHAKE IT OUT

It is time again to put the book down and allow all the words that have entered our minds to settle down and find a space to call home.

The following two exercises will give those thoughts the time to do just that. By focusing now on the sensations rather than the subjects, you will be able to experience a little of what Chi feels like, both from a physical and a mental perspective.

1. Stand erect and relaxed.
2. Begin to shake just one wrist as if shaking water off your fingertips, letting the wrist and fingers become completely limp in the process.
3. Then let the elbow go loose and shake the whole forearm, as well as your hand and fingers.
4. Now let go of your shoulder and shake that as well, as if your whole arm were a length of rope that you are trying to shake loose from your body.
5. After one minute of shaking, stop and just relax. Close your eyes and sense the difference between your two arms, hands, palms, and fingers.
6. Move the shaken arm around and notice the difference in the quality of the movement and in its relation to the air that passes around it.
7. Touch something or someone with each arm and notice any difference.

8. Then shake the other arm to balance yourself out.

WORKSHOP 6: FINDING YOUR RHYTHM

1. In the basic stance, stand with your hands gently placed over your abdomen.
2. Gently rock back and forth. Keep your feet on the floor, shifting the weight between the front of the feet and the heels—just as you practised in the chapter on posture. Try closing your eyes and focusing your attention on the different sources of energy around you to feel, first, the warmth of the sunlight and then the contact of the wind on your skin.
3. Connect your breathing rhythm with the movement of your body.
4. Slowly reduce the rocking, but continue the breathing rhythm.
5. As you breathe in, imagine all the energy (sunlight, wind... use your imagination) entering your body and meeting at the point where your hands are in contact with your abdomen.
6. As you breathe out, imagine this concentrated energy gathering in the abdomen, glowing, pulsing, and growing.
7. Repeat steps 5 and 6 for at least three to five minutes.
8. Rest.

ASK THE TEAPOT:

Q: But in my style - The Taoist School of Quivering Thighs - we believe that anyone who doesn't practise the Squatting Bear Bowel Releasing Routine during a full moon will never be able to hurl a passing elephant across the road by emitting a powerful  **'fajin nose twitch.' My teacher would say that without this technique, your Tai Chi may as well be Bean Curd Boxing.**

A: My point exactly.

Q: Is there really a substance called Qi?

A: You don't need to believe in a substance called Qi for it be a useful conceptual tool in your practice. The idea of Qi provides a framework for understanding health and well-being. For example as a metaphor for the overall state of health, encompassing physical, mental, and emotional well-being. Just as Western medicine considers factors like stress, diet, and exercise as part of overall health, Qi represents the balance and flow of these elements in the body.

Qi also can represent the concept of bio-electricity—the electrical processes that occur in the body, such as nerve impulses and cell signalling. In this way, the emphasis on movement and posture in Tai Chi could relate to biomechanics, where "good Qi" might equate to efficient, balanced body mechanics.

Q: Or are you just selling us more bean curd recipes?

A: One thing we learn when we look around at the health and spiritual practices of other cultures is that, unlike our own predominantly anatomical and analytical health care system with its methodologies based exclusively on the visible, the dissectible, and the observable, there exists a much wider global framework for health care—a framework that incorporates rather than excludes, that listens rather than speaks, that pays attention to subjective experience rather than dismissing it. Focusing only on what is in front of your nose means that you will only ever see what is hanging on the end of your nose. Which, of course, can be handy at times should something unpleasant be hanging there, but for most of the time it is recommended to cast your view a little wider. Remember the finger pointing to the moon?

Q: Which finger?

A: The one that distracted you from all the heavenly glory.

Q: That's as elusive to grasp as the Squatting Bear Bowel Releasing Routine.

A: Yes, it's a difficult one. The language we use is loaded with assumptions and preconceptions, so words in themselves can only take us so far in explaining these concepts. To be able to Do without Doing, we need to analyse less and go beyond the words.

Q: How can we go beyond words when all we have are the words in a book?

A: The words together just make up one finger. It's what the finger is pointing to that is important.

Q: Are we talking about the Moon again?

A: The moon, stillness, and the Embracing of Tigers.

FROM CHAOS TO STILLNESS:

EMBRACING YOUR TIGER

Stroll up to the things you most fear; get close, get so close that you can smell what they had for breakfast.

EMBRACING THE TIGER

As a young child on the streets of London, my two brothers and I were always looking for ways to earn money. We managed to do so through a number of semi-legal means, and with the proceeds we would indulge ourselves by buying armfuls of sweets and chocolates from the local confectioners. My favourite candy bar was called a Curly-Wurly, and it was only after first encountering this chocolate-covered toffee that I truly understood the wisdom of Bruce Lee, for left in the fridge overnight, a Curly-Wurly could be easily snapped in half and therefore shared among family members. Left in the sun for five minutes, however, and a Curly-Wurly becomes the softest thing on earth, unbreakable and consequently un-sharable. Softness, I learnt, had its advantages.

Softness was not difficult to find, even on the streets of South London, but stillness was as alien to me as an Alan Watts workshop on Emptiness would have been to my Welsh grandfather. Yet from my reading of Alan Watts, in the right circumstances, even stillness could be found where I lived. I would try to imagine Alan Watts meditating inside the courtyard of a Zen temple, his focused brow shaded by the dappled light filtering through the branches of an ancient cherry tree. A wind-chime sounds from afar, and a gentle wind rustles the dark red leaves above his head. A thrush provides a melodic mating song against the backdrop of a babbling brook; whilst Alan, meditating on the stiffness of a frozen Curly-Wurly, suddenly plunges his dusty feet into the cool water and gives them a long- overdue soak.

In such an environment, even a 24-hour social media addict would feel the temptation to disconnect and breathe a little deeper. But few of us then—or indeed now—have a handy Zen temple on the street corner. Where, then, are we to find such stillness while at work or on the move? Where does stillness reside in a world devoted to an ever- increasing pace? To find the answer, we will need to explore the idea of 'meditation in movement'. Meditation (stillness) and movement (activity) are two traditionally opposed concepts: In this apparent contradiction lies the essence of the next section - the co-existence of opposites or learning to Embrace the Tiger.

BEAN CURD BUSHIDO

There is a posture in Tai Chi called Embrace Tiger that conjures up one of the most important strategies of Bean Curd Boxing: three steps to embrace your enemy.

- The first step in Embrace Tiger involves strolling casually up to the things you most fear, rather than hiding from them. It is about moving in on their space, and then when you are staring them in the face, moving in closer still; so close that you can smell what they had for breakfast, taste the perspiration on their breath and count the hairs protruding from their nostrils.
- The second step necessitates the practice of Feet Breathing, so when you breathe out, you slowly smile and imperceptibly sink down to ground yourself.
- Finally, in step three, just as the look of shock begins to dissipate on the face of the tiger, gently turn, looking away only at the last moment, and still smiling, stroll slowly back home, following the grumblings of your stomach.

Through the adoption of such techniques, Bean Curd Boxing offers us the possibility of finding stillness in the centre of a busy city or whilst aboard a packed train during rush hour. Stillness can be found on the windiest of days, under the most threatening of skies and beneath the most torrential of onslaughts whether they are climatic or verbal. It is in these circumstances that we need to have with us our portable Zen temple, our very own path to stillness and the confidence to embrace all the tigers we meet en route.

TRAIN-SPOTTING AND MEDITATION

Many disciplines practice meditation to create a sense of space in otherwise cluttered and hectic lives. Although techniques vary from practice to practice, one popular method is to concentrate on letting go of the constant flickering images and thoughts that inhabit the mind. By neither holding on to thoughts nor chasing them from one place to another, you can learn to just let things be and, in so doing, a quietness of mind begins to develop all by itself. Then, if you wish, you can focus on particular feelings, specific thoughts, techniques, or just your breath.

In meditation, the aim is to stay alert yet open and quiet—not holding on to the incessant stream of data that passes through our conscious states, but learning to let it just pass by. Imagine you are standing on a train platform, awaiting the arrival of a specific train carrying a close friend who has come to visit you. While waiting, many other trains pass you by, but you do not scour each one, searching for a familiar face. You do not move from platform to platform, checking the arrival of each train. Nor do you return endlessly to the timetable boards to confirm the arrival time when you already know it. When the mind is able to focus on what is really relevant, you do not concern yourself with all the other stuff going on around you. The scenario is different, of course, for the trainspotters among you who may indeed find themselves glued to the arrival times display board, avidly scribbling down the seating capacity of the 6.35 to Paddington. But for most of us, it is about focus.

When practising the patterns and forms of Tai Chi and Bean Curd Boxing, the aim is to focus on what we are doing, or on nothing at all, while the body moves—following its own internal rhythms and engaging in the enigmatic duality of stillness and movement. Allow the trains to come and go, passengers to alight and board, but stay with what you are doing. Try practising this at a real train station: watch as people rush from one platform to another and fidget in anticipation of delays. Watch as they march militarily from one end to the other, uncomfortable with the notion of wait-ing, uncomfortable with this sudden serving of stillness in their otherwise busy lives. Now is the moment they need to Embrace their Tiger, to become part of everything and remain centred and rooted. As a Bean Curd Boxer, these exercises will provide you with all the tools you will need to start meditating in movement.

USING THE LIGHT SWITCH

To be able to successfully Embrace your Tiger and Meditate in Movement, it is necessary to practice: at train stations, in long and frustrating queues, or wherever stress and haste rear their familiar heads. On another, perhaps more important level, we can practice by letting go of expectations and the tendency to preview life before it happens. In other words, we can focus on our attitude.

If we watch our minds closely, we often see they have a tendency to overwork and get carried away: they play out worrying scenarios that have yet to occur or attempt to resolve problems by going over and over the same points. Consequently, we believe that by thinking something through thoroughly enough, we can resolve any issue or, at the very least, rehearse it enough times to handle whatever the real circumstances throw at us. Sometimes this is true, but not often. Instead, we project outcomes onto events that have yet to happen and, in so doing, initiate a set of circumstances that we expect to take place. As a result, we lose the reality of the moment and instead merely live out our own rehearsed version of life.

Bean Curd Boxers prefer to let go of all details and all projected scenarios and allow the mind to resolve everything in its own time and in its own way. Using just the mind to resolve issues is like using a searchlight to find a sock in the dark. With a searchlight, we can focus brightly on one area after another, but to get a broader view, the light switch is a far more useful option. When we start to use our bodies and our minds together, we are turning on the light switch.

Our attitude can often be the deci-  sive factor in how we interpret success or failure. The attitude of the Bean Curd Boxer's training comes from the rich history of Taoism—the set of ideas that generate the movements of Tai Chi. It is a curious philosophy because its ultimate expression is not written, nor spoken, but rather embraced (a technique we have already practised with the tigers in our lives). Taoism can be read about, discussed, and debated, but ultimately it has to be lived with a gentle force in order to be really comprehended. Hence, Bean Curd Boxing is a superb opportunity not just to learn a series of exercises for physical health but also to gain insight into another way of looking at and interacting with the world.

Our attitude, then, is fundamental to the success of all the techniques and exercises that we learn. It is an attitude that embraces not just tigers but also ideas about letting things go and leaving them undone. One of the most important ideas to let go of is the notion of absolutes and coherence. Bean Curd Boxers believe that anyone attempting to seek absolutes is, in the very act of seeking, stepping further from the path. In other words, the desire to achieve perfection is enough to keep one from achieving it.

In our daily lives, we are constantly bombarded through advertising with images of 'the perfect lifestyle' that we should aim to attain. Consumerism always promises satisfaction but rarely delivers. Our task, therefore, is to recognise this pattern and, instead of merely repeating it, to develop the capacity to enjoy more from less; to develop the capacity, for example, to distinguish subtle flavours, smells, and tastes from simple foods; to bathe in fresh waters and winds; to share simple pleasures with friends and family; and to readjust our notions of wealth to include qualities other than just the ability to out-consume our neighbours. In the next chapter, we shall look at some of the ways a Bean Curd Boxer can apply the principles of Taoism to the 21st-century world.

ASK THE TEAPOT:

Q: What's wrong with consuming our way through life? The entire planet has been built on this fine principal.

A: The accumulation of the stuff has its limits. At some point you'll end up tripping over all the useless gadgets in your home, and then you'll realise you need to do a course on decluttering or buy a book on how to recycle that unused home gym in the basement. This is not a meaningful way to pass through our brief time on this planet.

Q: It doesn't make me shallow just because I own 6 yachts....

A: Of curse not, but everything comes down to intention. Should you decide to convert those yachts into floating shelters for seagulls in need, then...

Q: But some things are simply black or white! Right or wrong! Good or evil!

A: All these are within us, to some extent. Right and wrong often depend on context, intentions, and perspectives. Kindness is universally a good thing, while causing harm is universally frowned upon. But many situations are more nuanced. Life's like that – it's about balance, mindfulness, having a sense of humour and making choices that not only align with your values, but the well-being of those around you.

CHAPTER 9

THE TAO OF DUST MERGING:

THE WISDOM OF NOT-DOING

 "If nothing within you stays rigid, outward things will disclose themselves."

One rather gloomy afternoon, the 4th century BCE philosopher Chuang Tzu put down his smartphone and sighed. His mobile signal was faltering once more, and the small processor was struggling to keep up with the daily app updates on his somewhat limited data package. He cast a crestfallen gaze towards the hazy mountain peaks that emerged through the drizzle-grey rain clouds ahead of him and lifted his weary head. The Ten Thousand Things around him were still at play, the Mountain was as still as it had been the previous evening, and the Four Winds that blew before him seemed oblivious to the bandwidth concerns of man. Bending over, he sighed once more as he tied up the straps on his worn-out sandals, for it was time to leave behind all the confusion and chaos of life. Picking up the moon and tucking it under his arm, Chuang Tzu set forth to merge with the dust of the Tao.

DUST MERGING IN THE 21ST CENTURY

Since those fabled days, Dust Merging has long since fallen out of fashion in the West, being misunderstood—since the onset of the industrial revolution—as the irritating consequence of infrequent vacuuming. But true Dust Merging is about more than mere house-keeping alone. Sometimes, when I feed my dog, he will drop the morsel on the floor before eating it so that he can lick up a mouth full of dust to accompany the titbit. My dog sees the connection. There is a thread between the dust bag and our interconnectivity with the life of others, the dust of our neighbours, and the stellar particles that inhabit our own individual make-up. When we empty the vacuum bag into the compost heap, we are reminded that our birth into this "bag of skin and bones"—as our friend Alan Watts was prone to describe our state of being—is no more or no less than the cosmos recycling its own dust: the dandruff of the heavenly bodies as they shake themselves down.

From the rise and fall of this dust comes the cycle of life and death, the interplay of opposites, and the movement of the cosmos. This in turn generates a pattern of movement known as the Ten Thousand Things, the philosophy of Taoism*[1], and the basis for applying Bean Curd Boxing to our daily activities.

THE TAO OF LAO TZU

What then is Taoism? Out of curiosity, I googled the question and received 182,000 definitions, the very first being: "A Chinese sect claiming to follow the teaching of Lao Tzu but incorporating pantheism and sorcery in addition to Taoism." Claiming? Pantheism? Sorcery? I was as confused as that fabled sentry guard must have been at the gates of the Enchanted City when Lao Tzu approached one cloudy evening on the back of a weary ox while on his way to merge with the dust of the universe and leave behind the turmoil of the city. The sentry, immediately recognising the CEO and founder of 5th century Taoism, bravely posed the question that has remained on most people's lips for centuries since: What is Taoism?

---

1. Pronounced as though written with a D instead of a T. See References at end of book for more on spelling and pronunciation.

"Taoism," Lao Tzu reportedly said, adjusting his posture to the bony contours of his seat, "Taoism is...well, it's a bit like...sort of... you see..." Eventually, Lao Tsu knew that there was only one answer he could give: "Those who know, do not speak, those that speak, do not know."

In other words, Taoism transcends language. This of course leaves us with the conundrum of how to explain the inexplicable. How do we define Taoism when the nearer we get to it, the further we are away? One answer is to postpone for the moment our search for what it is, as we just get into the sort of pickle that the sentry found himself in. Instead, we ought to ask why it is still around today. What three reasons could explain why Taoism has endured so?

1. Taoism is a philosophy of change that has survived the centuries, not because it has been buried away in dusty tomes or cobwebbed vaults, but because it is like a book lying open on the kitchen table, ready to be consulted daily before preparing a tasty dish. The essential writings do not so much constitute a book, but rather a journal to engage with when the winds of change alter their direction (which they tend to do quite often).

2. Taoism is a philosophy of change that has transmigrated from Asia into Europe and the Americas. It still offers a fresh perspective on our relationships with time, change, and adaptability and remains remarkably flexible,

irreverent, and apparently irrepressible (a bit like Bean Curd Boxing).

3. Taoism is a philosophy that eschews stagnancy by going beyond words, gathering up its poetic principles, and dragging them out onto the street to test their functionality through its paramilitary wing: Bean Curd Boxing.

THE TAO OF GAZPACHO

Now that we have some idea as to why it has endured so long, we can go back to asking what Taoism is. One answer is to think of it as a bowl of Gazpacho. Made predominantly of tomatoes, peppers, garlic, and olive oil, this synergy of ingredients combines to produce a disease-fighting cocktail that not only cools the body but also enables it to absorb antioxidants more readily. Gazpacho is yet another example of science confirming the wisdom of popular culture.

Having lived in the Andalusian region for several decades, Gazpacho became as regular a part of my diet as morning tea would be to an English person. But for visitors, it was always a challenge to convince them of the varied qualities of this cold Spanish soup. Despite listing the ingredients and their respective benefits, guests would generally remain unexcited, opting instead for another coffee during the midday heat. However, when a cooling glass of this cold liquid was eventually served and the first mouthful had been swallowed, it became clear that some things do indeed transcend language.

The Tao of Gazpacho reveals that the separate parts of this philosophy can tell us a lot about the benefits of its practice, but mix them all together in a bowl and leave them in the fridge for a few hours, and you will see that Taoism has transformed itself into something else entirely.

Our first taste of Taoism can be likened to the play of contradictions that we touched upon earlier in the book. When opposites entwine—as in the Yin-Yang symbol—they do so not in a struggle for dominance, but rather in a mutual embrace of love.

YIN YANG SOUP

The instantly recognisable black and white circle dates from around the 11th century and, according to popular legend, originally depicted the dark or shady, and light or sunny sides of a mountain. As the sun shifted in its daily trajectory, yin became yang and vice versa. What is important, however, is not the accuracy of the story, but the notion of transition, as neither element can ever be fixed or rigid. Instead, each is in a constant state of transformation, each containing a part of the other, each creating the seed of its opposite.

Shady, winter, and female. Sunny, summer, and male. Although we use words to define, separate, and distinguish these characteristics, they are, in fact, bonded together in mutual harmony and coexistence. One is defined by the degree to which the other is present or absent.

For the Bean Curd Boxer, the Yin Yang concept embraces the idea of positive difference, the idea of contradiction and change, and the idea of the harmony of opposites. This minimalist circle contains the fundamental mutuality of all things: Not only does each thing become its opposite, but all things are dependent on their opposites in an interconnected and interdependent world.

In other disciplines, this interplay of contradictions would be defined as a weakness, but in Bean Curd Boxing, it becomes a strength due to the recognition that without one, the other loses vitality and meaning. In both the movements of Tai Chi and the principles of Taoism, softness, vulnerability, yielding, and passivity are all employed to better one's health and to balance— or overcome when necessary—the hardness, defensiveness, resistance, and excessive activity of modern living.

For the keen Feet Breathers and the active Dust Mergers of the world, contradictions have a useful place, away from the old world of straight lines and rigid compatibilities. When the world is seen to be made up of lines—the line of cause and effect, the battle lines between states, the date line of history, or the washing line of dustless living—the subtle interweaving of relationships and processes remains invisible. In a Yin-Yang world, under the soft glare of the Bean Curd Boxer, incidents in life are the consequence of the interplay of contradictions that continuously swirl around us, evolving and producing new forms as we gently tread our personal paths. In this world, nothing is fixed; everything is in transition, everything decays, everything continues.

2. A WARMING CUP OF TE

Our second ingredient is something called Te, part of the classic book on Taoist philosophy by Lao Tzu (he of the Ox and the Enchanted City Gate). The Tao Te Ching is composed of several sections, the first being Tao Ching, or the classic book of the Way, and the second being the Te Ching, or the classic book of Virtue. The Tao Te Ching—more a series of scripts than a book—has been dated to approximately 300 BC, and although there has been consistent debate over whether Lao Tzu was really born old and lived to 990 years of age and whether he was in fact the author at all, we shouldn't let an absence of historical data get in the way of a really good story.

For those of you unfamiliar with the great book, I cannot recommend enough getting hold of a copy. It plays joyfully with ideas of passivity, creation, and the usefulness of emptiness, among other themes, and has become one of the great reference points for Westerners who wish to follow a life of voluntary simplicity and harmony in action. I have added a few of my favourite versions at the end of this book.

For the Bean Curd Boxer looking to add the concept of Te to their urban utility belt, it is necessary to grasp a broader definition than simply that of virtue. Te encompasses a range of internal characteristics that enable us to follow a given path: identity, personality, expression, conscious action, charisma, life force, etc. Te includes not just the talents and abilities we were born with, but also those that we learn en route, and even our ability, or means, of learning.

In simple terms, think about not just doing something well, but doing it appropriately and elegantly. Consider how the first mobile phones functioned before the advent of the smartphone. Those early designs were unintuitive, clumsy, and frustrating to use. Then, one company decided to remove functions instead of adding them.

It is difficult to argue that a piece of technology can have Te, but when it addresses the way we learn and guides us in reaching new goals, we can begin to see Te in action.

As Bean Curd Boxers, therefore, we are left with a truly exciting challenge: Can that to which we devote our lives be addressed with virtue, or Te? It should never be enough to just approach a project or task from the mere perspective of functionality, but with simplicity and character too. If we combine Te with the lessons of grounding, breathing, and energy sensibilities, we start to amass a powerful toolkit for the Urban Seeker of Curves.

3. SOME GENTLY FRIED FISH

Our third ingredient is probably one of the most important elements in Taoism, and in the whole discipline of Bean Curd Boxing. It is called Wu Wei and has a lot to do with the careful cooking of fish. Lao Tzu wrote that looking after your affairs is the same as cooking a small fish; too much prodding and fussing in the frying pan and the meal will end in ruins. This is the essence of Wu Wei. It is found in the confidence to let things take their course, to know when to act and when to let things be. Followers of Wu Wei work alongside the forces of nature, employing a soft and flexible spatula when dealing with worldly affairs so that all action appears as non-action.

Other than the prodding of fish, it has been the yielding nature of water that has best symbolised the essence of Wu Wei. However, even this classic metaphor has been challenged by that of A.A. Milne's Pooh Bear, who—thanks to Benjamin Hoff's excellent book: The Tao of Pooh—has come to represent a more familiar icon for the art of effortless doing.

Pooh's idea of Wu Wei is that the universe works best when left alone to find its own harmony and balance. Effort is the result of working out of step with this process, which in turn creates greater disharmony and the need for yet more effort. Thus, the more Rabbit, Owl, or Eeyore intervene in the workings of the forest, the less is achieved. It is Pooh's detachment and reluctance to engage with effort that permits him to act only when it is appropriate. Consequently, though he appears to do little, he is in fact the bear that Gets Things Done.

There are many parallels in the world of productivity where companies and individuals break down their agendas into contextual tasks, projects, and sub-tasks. This approach encourages the emptying of your head of everything that needs doing—no matter how small the project—into an organised filing system: tiresome thoughts, unfinished tasks, upcoming calendar dates, and anything else that still needs doing. But for the followers of Wu Wei,  such organisational tools only bequeath an endless list that must be tackled again at a later date. Head emptying is a wonderful practice, but not if it merely postpones the refilling until the following morning. For Wu Wei, once a project or task is recognised as needing to be done, it should be left alone. The subconscious will work on a path forward; meanwhile, the best thing an individual could do is to detach themselves: Go and plant some herbs, cook a dhal with plenty of garlic, or take the dog out for a walk

4. VOLUNTARY SIMPLICITY

 "Can anything be so elegant as to have few wants, and to serve them one's self?" — Ralph Waldo Emerson

Our final ingredient is a complementary addition to that of Wu Wei, for it focuses once more on non-interference and the attempt to work in accordance with nature. When we interfere with the natural course of movement—or perhaps better said—when we interfere without awareness in this process, we create effort. Two local examples spring to mind:

95

EXAMPLE ONE:

I once lived in a village on the Mediterranean coast, where the rocky and stony beaches were small and befitting an unimposing fishing town. Then the town council decided one year that it was to be no longer just a fishing town, for it dreamt of developing itself into a grand tourist resort. To develop the town's rather meagre, but sustainable, scale of tourism, they decided to extend the main beaches to accommodate more sunbathers during the summer season. Thereafter, each winter, convoys of trucks dumped a mixture of soil and fine sand onto the stony beaches. Each year, the exercise was repeated and each year the tides immediately washed most of it out to sea. With what soil remained, some canny locals planted potatoes, and by early summer a wonderful crop sprang up amongst the sun-loungers and parasols. It appeared that politics and money, when they got together, just had to interfere with nature.

EXAMPLE TWO:

Over the same period, just as the town had picked its unexpected potato glut, a plague of jellyfish turned up in its waters during the peak of the tourist season to idly float about among desperate bathers and feed on floating layers of waste materials.

The jellyfish had not come to sun bathe or rest their tentacles on a deckchair, but rather for the effluent that was pumped out into the shallow waters further along the coast by the extensive residential and commercial conurbations that had been developed over the last decade. As sea temperatures warmed and the natural enemies of the jellyfish were gradually wiped out by overfishing, these stinging, translucent invertebrates were pretty much left to their own devices, resulting in thousands of tourists stranded on the shore's edge during the high season.

According to the rules of Edward Bear and Voluntary Simplicity, if you do not understand the principle of working with nature, then all you do is create more work for yourself. This, of course, does not mean that you never interfere nor manipulate nature; rather, you do so with the knowledge and awareness of the rhythms and cycles of her language. Voluntary Simplicity states that with such knowledge we can all learn better how to interrelate with one another as well as with Mother Nature. If we do not follow these rules, then like our coastal examples, Mother Nature will interfere with us. Voluntary Simplicity recommends that we learn to do with less and experience life in a way that is outwardly simple but inwardly rich. It promotes a way of life that embraces minimal consumption, minimal environmental damage, and presents a philosophy of living and working with others in a less competitive way.

Voluntary Simplicity takes many ideas, from Thoreau to Gandhi, and blends them together with the concepts of Yin-Yang and Wu Wei. It supports the Slow Movement by encouraging us all to decelerate and downsize our lives so that we leave less of a footprint in a world that has yet to learn the lessons of finite resources and the importance of sustainability. Like Lao Tzu in the Tao Te Ching, the movement stresses that it is not what we do that is so important, but rather what we should not do that will determine the quality of our time and our relationships.

ASK THE TEAPOT:

Q: I'm not sure I understand the idea of Voluntary Simplicity from the jellyfish and sand stories. Can you give me another example?

A: An often-cited example is that of contamination: For a cleaner environment, would it be more efficient to buy more brooms or throw less rubbish on the floor? In the case of the jellyfish, the Town Council chose to deal with the symptoms rather than the cause and thereby expended greater effort. They hired boats each summer to skim the jellyfish up in nets, they employed beach patrols to stop bathers entering the water, and equipped the health centres with additional medicines to treat the increase in jellyfish stings. Despite such efforts, restaurants and hotels watched as tourists—prohibited from cooling off in the August heat—cut short their holidays and headed inland.

Q: It all sounds far too simplistic. Are you saying if we gave up polluting the environment, the environment wouldn't be polluted?

A: It might help.

Q: And that would mean not doing something in order to do something. In this case, save the planet. Yes?

A: Ehm, well, yes. To do without doing is the general idea.

Q: But if, for example, we stopped flying, then it will take a greater effort to get anywhere! Am I right or am I right?

A: We are clearly moving towards a transport system not based on fossil fuels, so this may require us to rethink the purpose of journeying and the present addiction to doing so in as short a time as possible. Maybe we will rediscover the pleasure of taking time over travel, even consider the use, once more, of our legs.

Q: I quite like the idea of using my legs again. And downsizing appeals, but there have to be limits. I do not want to give up my mobile phone, for example.

A: It is likely that access to unlimited information will not be the ultimate consumable item forever. At some point, simple wisdom and intuition will have to take over from mere data exposure. Then, we will all need to ask ourselves whether it is quantity or quality that we seek.

Q: When you talk about change and not doing; about acting in accordance with nature or the Way, how does the process begin? Is it a mental or physical shift first?

A: The shift comes as you align yourself.

Q: Align myself with what? Conspiracy theories? Facebook bots following me around?

A: Could be, but more likely with your breath.

Q: Are we back to Feet Breathing again?

A: Did we ever leave it?

Q: This is all too evasive. I really need to know how to shift from an idea or an item on my to-do list, to a state of productivity. How do I get from thought to action?

A: Have you tried typing it into Google Maps?

Q: No!

A: Then don't. Turn off the mobile phone. Adopt the basic posture, breathe as you have been shown, let your mind settle, and follow what happens. Bean Curd Boxing is not rocket science. Think of it as discovering yourself on Facebook and smiling that you are back in touch with an old friend. When you learn how to trust your body and mind working together, and you don't censor what comes up, then answers to such questions arise every day. Get used to the process because it will happen a lot from now on. Just follow it, and, as it emerges, decide where you want to go with it. But let the process take place, for, if not, it festers and seeps out just when you are showering the dog, composting the egg carton, or capturing the flight of a humming bee. And then, you are back to where you started.

Q: But what if all this...philosophy, this way of being...what if it's all just words?

A: That is all it is.

Q: Then, how do I know if these words correspond to anything real?

A: If nothing within you stays rigid, outward things will disclose themselves. In moving, be like water. In stillness, be like a mirror. Respond like an echo.

Q: Who said that? Gandhi?

A: No, Lee.

Q: Christopher?

A: Bruce.

THE ART OF LOSING:

THE UNCLENCHED FIST

Before you know it, a modern day assassin will have moved in and taken up residence on the sofa.

Themselves building blocks of Bean Curd Boxing are found in good posture and body mechanics, breath, energy, and the Wu Wei approach to problem-solving. But many new to the art ask, "Where is the Boxing in the Bean Curd?" To what degree are the internal martial arts expressed externally? Should the martial, like the romantic anachronism of the sword-wielding ninja, be confined to the storylines of Asian cinema screens? To find the answer to these questions, we will be investigating the ancient practice of Losing in Order to Win.

Today's masked assassin wears a more subtle disguise than that of a black-garbed ninja and is concealed far more effectively than hiding on a pagoda rooftop. Today's assassin is found hidden amongst the lifestyles and habits of the city dweller, and it is there that Bean Curd Boxing must do battle.

Bean Curd Boxers have long argued that the balance of the world has changed. Our society has become—in Taoist terms—overtly Yang. The global economy, based on rampant, open competition, has become the common reference point for alliances, both economic and political. When these alliances are threatened or weakened, embargoes, invasion, war, and regime change are used to reinstate this increasingly fragile economic model. On a local scale, population density, finite resources, and food and water scarcities contribute towards a clear deficiency of Yin, leaving society unbalanced and ill at ease with itself and the direction it travels. To practice Bean Curd Boxing in such a world—a world that cries out for balance—requires a contextual rethink from all martial artists.

Martial arts have many varied benefits, of which only some are martial in application. Personal discipline, spiritual ideas, mind-body training, and energy channelling, to name but a few.

However, the value of the martial applications is rooted in other times and other cultures. Today, society has moved away from a world where each individual was obligated to defend themselves, their family, and the national borders of their state. The Chinese Boxer Rebellion at the end of the 19th century clearly showed the limits of that particular approach. We shall return to this subject a little later.

Some argue that the full name of Tai Chi—Tai Chi Chuan—signifies the essence of martial in the art, as "Chuan" means "fist." However, "Chuan" in Mandarin can also mean "to pass on" or "to transmit," as used in contexts like traditions or stories being passed down.

For Bean Curd Boxers, the Chuan in Tai Chi Chuan is found elsewhere than in the reflexive clenching of a fist. If we look further into the depth of our root, our ability to keep our centre, and move with coordinated limbs and breath, there we will find real strength. Keeping our fists clenched will only  mean that we can never offer a supporting hand to others. Therefore, before leaving home, Bean Curd Boxers make sure they have unclenched their fists, teeth, and muscles. They believe that modern-day assassins are less likely to be found in dark and uninviting alleyways but rather on supermarket shelves, cleverly disguised as modified food. They are to be found in fast food outlets, posing as quick and healthy alternatives, or in the waste pipes of chemical companies that discharge contaminated residues into our rivers and oceans. For the Bean Curd Boxer, the thoroughly modern assassin must be fought with different weapons and on different battlefields. If we do not let go of the old ideas of who the enemy really is, we are more likely to meet our end at the hands of supermarket additives, rather than by the swing of a samurai's sword.

 In martial arts, the most powerful move is the one you never need to make. Leave it undone—let the universe handle the heavy lifting.

Whatever the conclusions of the Great Martial Debate, there are still some useful training drills that any practitioner of Bean Curd Boxing should heartily embrace. These include the classic "Four Small Steps to Keeping Your Bean Curd Firm," as well as the Push Hands training program to combat a subtle and clever assailant we know as The Confirmation Bias. By training ourselves in these manoeuvres, we will learn not only how to overcome these modern assassins, but also acquire the ancient skill of losing in order to win.

Some assassins come running at us in full black garb, wielding a knife, a pistol, or aiming a rubber bullet at our chest. These are the easy ones to deal with. They rely on brute force, numbers, and predictable movements. Others, however, sneak quietly up behind us and slip down our shirt when we're smoking a cigarette, eating a bacon sandwich, or scratching our bottom whilst shaking hands with the mayor. They then settle into a pleasant life at our side, and before we know it, they have moved in and taken up the sofa.

These modern day vigilantes eventually turn into bad habits, and the problem with bad habits is that they tend to seek corroboration from the world around us, like an echo on your Facebook timeline. For example, in our arguments, we tend to seek out those who can corroborate the opinions and attitudes we already hold. Rarely do we seek out arguments that may contradict our firmly held beliefs. Smokers hang out with other smokers, and baconsarnie addicts with like-minded others. In this way, we back up our beliefs and further entrench our worldviews and habits. This tendency is known as The Confirmation Bias, and in Tai Chi, we look to challenge this tendency in the practice of Push Hands.

PUSH HANDS

Push Hands is a traditional component of Tai Chi that has its roots in martial applications, but, unlike other practices, it has evolved

over time into an exercise for
exploring imbalances, vulnerabili-
ties, and blockages of both mental
and physical origins. The exercise
consists of a series of simple pushes
and corresponding yields that
expose an individual's scratching
and munching tendencies.

The aim of each push is not to
topple or unbalance your partner—though this too often occurs in
public competitions—but rather to encourage awareness of bad
habits through their continuous exposure. This practice provides a
rare opportunity to focus on and explore our responses with a co-
operative partner.

For example, there may be a reluctance to yield on one side or a
resistance to actually push a partner. These physical patterns may
suggest an inflexibility: a reticence to applying force. Thus,
through the magnifying glass of Push Hands, we learn to become
aware of our habits in our daily interactions. It is not an easy exercise, and many students either resent the slowly surfacing confirmation bias or simply use force to hide its appearance. It is the
teacher's role to demonstrate that it is often only through the
study of slow repetition that bad habits come to our attention.
Once exposed, we can decide how best to let them go.

"Invest in loss" is the guiding principle of Push Hands. The aim is
to gain by not winning. We have to learn from both the disclosure
of weaknesses and the process of losing. The difficulty lies in the
tendency to be defensive and the desire to win, but vulnerability
and exposure teach us a lot about ourselves and how to avoid old

patterns and routines. Push Hands is a fine method for learning to deal with the assassins that are still occupying the sofa.

ASK THE TEAPOT

Q: Are you saying that Tai Chi is not a martial art?

A: There are many elements that would be useful to those training in martial arts, such as balance and coordination work, breathing control, muscle relaxation and yielding skills, grounding, and rooting. However, these would need to be taught alongside, for example, the groundwork in Brazilian Jiu-Jitsu and the fist and knee sparring in Thai Boxing.

Q: Because?

A: As Mike Tyson said:

 Everyone has a plan until they get punched in the face.

Q: Meaning?

A: Watch any of the bouts in China between Mixed Martial Artists and traditional Tai Chi Masters, and you'll see why Tyson's advice is pertinent.

Q: Well, I've seen videos of Tai Chi Masters throwing students across the room without even touching them! Are you saying that's just Bullshido?

A: I'm saying YouTube has a lot to answer for.

Q: In our Tai Chi Martial Arts School, we spend hours each week hardening our fists, doing bag work, and sparring full-contact. Don't you understand that you have to be ready at any moment to defend King and country, and your home and family when the time comes?

A: Developing callouses on your knuckles in order to have an 'Iron Fist,' only to find yourself getting Tasered in your first street confrontation, strikes me as a dubious pastime. Did we not learn anything from the Boxer Rebellion?

Q: I can see that the only way we'll resolve our differences is in the ring.

A. Sigh.

CATS, FLAMINGOS, TORTOISES, AND TARZAN:

A BEAN CURD BOXER'S GUIDE TO URBAN SERENITY

Be like a cat my friend: move with stealth, glare with purpose, and stalk your goals like they're made of tuna.

A s Push Hands, like all martial applications, is an interactive exercise requiring a series of changing partners, you'll need to find someone you can practice with. Join a local class or take an online course with a friend. Failing that, grasp the principles and step out into your day with the aim of embracing the first tiger you meet.

Do not be dismayed however, if you should find that the more dogmatic martial practitioners of Tai Chi however, dismiss Push Hands as a true martial practice. They argue that only by studying the fighting applications of the Form will the Yang element of Tai Chi be truly present and the practice balanced. These practitioners argue that without these fighting moves, Tai Chi is just a series of slow-motion postures that are far too soft and yielding; not too dissimilar from bean-curd, in fact. Consequently, this version of Tai Chi has been labelled Bean-Curd Boxing, and Bean-Curd Boxers generally tend, as is their nature, to absorb such criticisms and just plod on.

Some, however, whose curd is perhaps a little less floppy, have tried to point out where modern battles arise and that Bean Curd Boxers do in fact still learn to fight—but fight with weapons other than clenched fists (though occasionally they may employ these too, should the circumstances necessitate). Bean Curd Boxers fight by Softening Their Glare, Banishing Frowns, and Slowing Down when asked to speed up. Bean Curd Boxers do not toss shurikens —hidden circular swords tossed like Frisbees at approaching enemies—but instead discharge smiles, and when backed into a corner, they come out fighting with well-aimed tales of nonsense and contradiction.

Whether your aim is to develop the five-finger death touch or simply to keep your Bean Curd from getting too limp, all practitioners agree that it is vital to learn how to apply Tai Chi outside the class. When in class, we experience inner tranquillity, spatial awareness, flow, and a powerful sense of being grounded. But as we leave the sanctuary of the classroom and return to the routine of our working lives, we are left with a sense of loss as to how to sustain the serenity and balance of the previous hour.

In the Manual of Bean Curd Boxing, there are four simple techniques for achieving this goal that will help integrate the lessons of the class and Keep Your Bean Curd Firm, and the first is to Walk like a Cat.

WALK LIKE A CAT

Continuity of movement is one of the most noticeable components of Tai Chi, and together with the breathing techniques, it is what differentiates the art from other health practices such as yoga.

 The difference between yoga and Tai Chi, is that even if you get it studying yoga, there's nothing you can do if someone tries to knock you off your cushion.

— WOLFE LOWENTHAL

Tai Chi is movement, and in movement, we take our principles and ideas out for a test drive. We run them through the challenges of an urban landscape and see how well they fare. Through observing ourselves in movement, we come to see our inherited or acquired patterns as we interact and engage with the world, rather like the Push Hands exercise, but on a much grander scale.

Walk Like a Cat is an exercise in movement and sensitivity and adopts the legendary Chang San Feng's advice on life and immortality: hang around with animals and hope to absorb some of their qualities (more on Chang San Feng and his pets in the following chapter).

Walk Like a Cat, however, is not about imitating the purring, mouse-slaying, rubbish-rummaging qualities of our feline friends, but rather the elegant and focused gait of their movement.

Watch a cat hunt a bird or small rodent, and you will see an animal in an extraordinary state of balance, with coordinated limbs, measured breath, and focused concentration. How then do you Walk Like a Cat? Should you be old enough to remember David Carradine in the opening sequences of the 1970s cult series Kung Fu, then you will remember the intricate footsteps along the rice paper before he embraced the burning Shaolin urn. You will also undoubtedly remember his obligatory side-steps and shimmies conducted in candlelight before he was allowed to leave the temple. Well, forget all of that nonsense. This is the real thing.

WORKSHOP 7: WALK LIKE A CAT

1. Keep your head up high on your shoulders and look straight ahead.
2. Keep your centre of gravity low and your knees softly bent.

3. Do not lock your knees; keep the joints open.

4. Move one foot cautiously off the floor, peeling the sole of the foot slowly from the ground as though it were partially stuck with glue. Do not look at the floor or at your feet, but instead keep your eyes focused in front of you. This will help maintain your balance.

5. With one leg raised, begin to place the heel down in front of you, slowly.

6. With the heel now on the ground, roll the rest of the foot forward towards the toes.

7. Keep your arms relaxed and at your sides, and do not hold your breath!

8. Keep the breathing slow and deep, and like the changing shift of weight and balance, keep it all in constant movement.

9. The upper body must be light, soft, and yielding, able to turn and shift as circumstances dictate.

Breathe easily and relax, but do not go into some strange meditative state or start chanting anything. This will just frighten neighbours, other walking cats, and visiting relatives. On the contrary, stay calm, quiet, and focused like a hunting feline, and stay conscious of what is happening all around you. Cat walking is not just about balance and poise, but increasing alertness whilst relaxing and staying on the move.

TARZAN'S FEET

Let's consider another example of cat walking, and ask our old friend the Earl of Greystoke to come back and help us again. Remember all those times he would run barefoot through the jungle as fast as a speeding gazelle? He would leap over rotting trees, wave at the king of the beasts, shimmy around dozing hippos, and then just as he was about to reach a struggling Jane, who had been fighting off a band of foreign animal poachers, Tarzan would run straight into some cleverly concealed elephant pit with stakes protruding upwards from the ground.

Now, had the Lord of the Apes been practising Cat Walking instead of galloping frivolously beneath the green canopy, his cautious heel-to-toe steps would have detected the false banana leaves covering the spiky pit long before he had transferred all his weight unconditionally into the very centre of the pit. Consequently, the evil animal poachers would have received their comeuppance, and Tarzan would have remained un-spiked. However, some of you may argue that by practising Cat Walking, Tarzan would never have rescued Jane. I can but request that you refrain from commenting until you reach Step 3: Drive Like a Tortoise.

OUT AND ABOUT

Once the basic steps of Cat Walking have been mastered at home, head out to your nearest supermarket and boldly enter the busiest aisle you can find. Apply the lessons learned above and make a note of what happens around you; move in on open spaces; glide away from trolleys as they loom in front of you. Use your peripheral vision to observe distracted shoppers scrutinising food labels or studying incoming text messages on mobile devices whilst blindly steering a loaded shopping trolley. Always move from your centre, and always take your centre with you. Never leave it at home or in the car, or back there in the fruit and vegetable aisle. Never permit it to wander off by itself. Stay centred, and that way if someone does knock into you, you can yield softly, throw out a shuriken smile, and move on. Keep your centre of balance low so that the upper body can yield to all things that move into your space. This is the aim of Cat Walking: to consciously stay calm whilst consumerist chaos surrounds you.

Once you feel sufficiently accomplished in the supermarket aisle, try the same exercise at a busy street market. For a real balance challenge, board a crowded rush-hour train and make your way to the buffet carriage. Buy a hot coffee and resist the urge to put a plastic lid on top (think about all those fish-choking, floating plastic islands in the middle of the ocean). Then try to make your way back to your seat without spilling hot coffee on your trousers or on those of other passengers.

STAND LIKE A FLAMINGO

Flamingos need no lessons in balance. They habitually sleep on one leg, minimising temperature loss in the shallow waters beneath their feet, and when tired, they simply change from one damp limb to another. If Chang San Feng had been a little more of a pirate and a little less of a landlubber, he may  even have adopted a flamingo rather than an orangutan. We shall return to Chang in the next chapter.

In Steps 1 and 2, it is necessary to have a good sense of balance, but what do we mean by balance? Although many belief systems engage metaphysically with the notion of balance, few provide us with the tools for its development. Bean Curd Boxing, however, does just that by developing the strength of the ligaments and the concept of rootedness. We first looked at rooting at the beginning of this manual in the section on posture. Having a root can be the difference between staying up or crashing down. In my back garden, there is a large fruit tree that serves to give shade and privacy throughout the year. It also produces a fruit - a small orange coloured fruit not unlike an apricot. Inside this fruit are four or five large pips that, if gathered and nonchalantly tossed into an earth-filled pot, miraculously produce small shoots. Encouraged by the ease of reproducing plants, I then go on to try and transplant them into the garden, but find that the majority die very quickly. It appears that those that survive have managed to establish roots, whilst those that flop over during the first light breeze have proven unsuccessful in establishing deep connections.

If we have no roots with which to anchor ourselves while the seas of change forever lap at our feet, then we too will fall at the first sign of an oncoming storm. In the art of Bean Curd Boxing, we learn to root ourselves in motion, so that when the bad weather does come, we will be well-practised in the art of Standing Like a Flamingo.

WORKSHOP 8: STAND LIKE A FLAMINGO TO ADD YEARS TO YOUR LIFE

1. Leg Lifting

- Practice initially by lightly holding on to a chair or pillar.
- Lift one leg slightly off the ground.
- The knee of the supporting leg should be soft and open to

allow the weight to be carried by your large thigh muscles.

- Keep your head up, back straight, and look directly ahead.
- Drop your shoulders, elbows, and chest.
- Hold the posture and then rotate your ankle joint slightly one way, then the other.
- Repeat with your knee, and then change legs.

Practice the balance exercise at least three or four times a day while you are doing something else, such as brushing your teeth or waiting for the kettle to boil. You might be standing in line at the bank, in a bus queue, or anywhere that you have a moment to regain your balance.

2. Stairs and Escalators

When climbing or descending stairs (going down stairs is an underrated, yet immensely beneficial exercise), take each stair at half your normal pace, avoiding locking the knees to prolong the one-legged moment.

This will slowly strengthen your joint ligaments, giving you greater tensile strength as well as greater confidence in your gait, your stance, and ultimately your notion of what constitutes good balance. Do not try this on metro escalators during rush hour, or you may find other commuters unappreciative of your training regime. There are, however, other exercises to do whilst on the underground.

3. Tubes, Metros, and Undergrounds

Take the tube during rush hour carrying a cup of water without a lid (this way, no one will be scalded by slopping coffee). As the train begins to move, stand still, focus on one object with your head held high, and then just slip one foot marginally off the floor. If you feel you may be losing your balance, adjust your weight and keep your joints open until you have no option but to place the foot back on the floor. Then repeat again and again. When practising, if you remember to keep your foot raised just a few centimetres off the ground, it will be easier to replace it when you begin to lose balance. Additionally, fellow passengers will be less likely to report you to the counter-terrorist police as a suspicious commuter standing on one leg and carrying a potentially dangerous liquid.

Some students, to further develop this training program, have tried standing for long periods in soggy marshlands or a deep puddle on the street during an autumnal downpour. This is not to be recommended as, although we aim to Stand Like a Flamingo, we try not to duplicate where a flamingo may stand.

WHERE CAN BALANCE BE FOUND?

Balance is found not just in the ligaments of the legs; it is present in the patterns of breath, in the confidence of an urban stride, or in the smiles that are distributed with the accuracy of a shuriken.

Balance is found in the language of shape and form, and in the arguments and opinions that float past us at the bus stop, as we wait, one foot inconspicuously an inch from the ground.

Balance is in the recognition that all things have two sides, two aspects, or two poles that—although opposite in nature—differ only by degree.

Balance is found in learning to recognise the circularity of extreme points, as they reach out and touch each other, shake hands, and merge.

Balance for the Bean Curd Boxer is in a permanent state of flux—an Orwellian perspective worth remembering when you next catch sight of your life-long nemesis.

DRIVE LIKE A TORTOISE

In previous chapters we have explored the need to embrace the philosophy of slow movements. Here, we will explore specific examples of how to apply Bean Curd Boxing to the notion of speed in our daily activities. Driving a vehicle  presents us with many opportunities to apply the lessons from this Manual of Bean Curd Boxing. Questions of speed, the behaviour of other drivers, and our reactions all serve as a fertile training ground for Keeping Your Bean Curd Firm.

Speed has a habit of accelerating more than just our travel time. It affects our judgments of urgency, priority, and safety. Think how slow traffic appears as you merge onto the slip road from the motorway at 100 kph, and how slow everything seems as you reluctantly adjust to urban speed limits. When we travel slowly, we notice details. When we travel fast, details blur. One example of this phenomenon is seen in city driving, where the surprising fact is that slower speeds can ensure a quicker arrival.

This intriguing contradiction has been observed in several studies of traffic patterns in busy cities. One such study, a 2011 report from the University of West England and Toyota Manufacturing UK, found that driving at consistent moderate speeds improved traffic flow more than attempting to drive faster in dense conditions. There appears to be an optimal speed for city traffic—driving faster than this speed results in more traffic jams, more congestion, more frustrated and impatient drivers, and consequently, slower-moving traffic.

WORKSHOP 9: DRIVE LIKE A TORTOISE

Impatience behind the wheel of a car is counterproductive. If someone has been driving behind you for the last five miles at a distance of just four inches, do not get impatient or annoyed. Instead, grasp the opportunity to practice Bean Curd Boxing and claim the moment as a free lesson.

- Begin by reacting to your reaction: Where has your attention shifted? Is it on the road or the vehicle behind?
- Note how you are grasping the steering wheel and ask yourself where all that tension came from.
- Notice whether you feel annoyed, irritated, or endangered. Then let go of it all and relax, for what's really important is not what others are doing (since others will always do things outside your control) but rather your chosen response.

- Try laughing at the absurdity of the things we all do under stress: the risks we take, the tension we build up, and the displaced anger that we then have to deal with. When you feel yourself tightening up—teeth clenched, frothing at the mouth, and about to pull down the window to toss out a real shuriken at a passing driver— wait just a moment and look at yourself. It's you out there too.

- Instead of reacting this way, search for where the tension is accumulating in your body (usually in the shoulders and arms), and then take just one long, slow breath. Remember, Bean Curd Boxers unclench their fists, teeth, and frowns when leaving home.

The answer sounds easy, perhaps too easy for an urban warrior who feeds on clashes and conflict. If this is you and you feel tempted to just stop the car and leap out, wielding the wheel brace over your head, try something else: slow driving. Slow down and let others pass, and as they accelerate at warp speed, smile and wave because you know you were like that once yourself— before you realised how unflustered you can live this life.

Slowing down not only speeds things up but also offers the benefit of enjoying the journey once more. You notice people and begin to take notice of the climate and the environment that you habitually passed by. Do not cut yourself off from what is around you; instead, open yourself to all of it. Perhaps this sounds like a small and insignificant detail, but it is one of the most important and life-changing benefits of practising a slow art like Bean Curd Boxing.

At home, our aim is to slow down so that we can observe the minutiae, the fine details of what happens as we move from one activity to another. When we look at the Tai Chi Form carefully, we see that there is not a series of postures after all, but rather a series of flowing, circular movements with no gaps and no pauses. There is no end or beginning. The Form is not unlike any other activity or any other means of travel. Look closely, and you will find that everything is interconnected. By travelling fast, this thread becomes almost invisible. Slow down, and it becomes a link, a guide, and a path.

WORKSHOP 10: SOFTEN YOUR GLARE

The organised chaos and hectic pace of life in the city have taught us many important and useful things, but often at the expense of tranquillity, clean air, personal space, and compassion. As a conse-quence, people have learned to deal with the negative aspects by shutting down a part of themselves, hardening their minds and bodies, and creating a portable wall between themselves and their everyday surroundings.

The telltale sign is in the eyes, which are incapable of hiding the real state of the soul. The glare of a city dweller is hardened by the harshness of what they have to look at every day: the things that must be ignored, the things that cannot be ignored, the things heard in bed at night, above the rush of the traffic-sirens that harden the muscles in the chest and restrict the flow of blood to the heart.

Over time, this hardening appears normal as city dwellers pass their time amongst each other, each confirming the bias of the other until it becomes only visible to non-city dwellers, who, upon pointing out the harshness of life in the great metropolis, are pooh-poohed by their city friends who have lost all means of recognising the symptoms. The practice of Push Hands and the "4 Steps to Keep your Bean Curd Firm" will help counter the glare of urban life, but the calcification of the spirit is an insidious process visible only through subtle telltale signs. While developing your skills of balance on the tube tomorrow morning, count the frowns and then count the smiles. See which is winning.

ASK THE TEAPOT:

Q: If suddenly I feel out of balance, what should I do first?

A: Balance is a term with many meanings. If you're experiencing a momentary imbalance, do a quick check: Has an earbud fallen out? Have you stood in something? Are both pedals operable? Has a heel come off?

Q: Other than talk, what can Bean Curd Boxing offer someone in need of life balance?

A: Always do a basic posture check first. You'll be surprised how often simple solutions can be found for simple problems. Then try standing on one leg, particularly when talking to someone—like the Mayor of your town, for example—and watch what happens.

Perfect balance won't happen overnight. It is a slow process, but going slow is, in itself, finding balance.

Q: Are the benefits of Slow Living slow to appear too?

A: What happens if you roll a snowball along the ground? If you stop rolling it after three feet and pull out your ruler to measure the difference, you'll see very little change. But if you keep rolling and stop a kilometre down the hill, you'll need to find something much larger than a ruler.

Q: Why is fast necessarily bad? What's wrong with microwave popcorn and Pot Noodles?

A: There's always a time and place for everything. Fast can be good too. The ideal is to be able to choose for yourself, and not have that decision made for you. As for the Pot Noodles...

Q: If I don't shout at other drivers on the road, what will happen to all my pent-up anger and frustration?

A: The secret is known as The Continuous Discharge. Notice how you respond to annoying things: the small increases in tension as your muscles tighten and the shortening of the breath will eventually make your driving more erratic. If you see froth bubbling from your lips and your knuckles on the steering wheel going white, these are signs. Employ The Continuous Discharge: loosen up and let go bit by bit, and watch how the stress evaporates.

Q: The Continuous Discharge then is just a way of loosening up?

A: Pretty much, yes. Lao Tzu said that we must learn to tackle the big things when they are small. So it's about developing an awareness of tension before it manifests as a muscle spasm or something worse. Ideally, you want to be able to choose how you live your life, so look for tightness and lack of movement in the joints, muscles, and mind. As soon as you notice those things, begin to loosen up before they become inflexible habits.

Q: I like the idea of Slow Driving, but as an ambulance driver, I'm not convinced that the patient in the back will appreciate my slowing down to point out the dappled sunlight of an overhanging cherry tree or to pull over to let an impatient driver pass by.

A: Speed sometimes needs to be grasped with both hands. But those hands need to be soft and relaxed so that decisions can be made with a calm spirit and not a tense, closed mind.

Q: I'm not sure about the implications or the practice of Step 4. How do I Soften my Glare?

A: When you only smile with your mouth, it shows. Try smiling with your eyes too, and watch how such a smile—a shuriken smile—will dissolve the frowns of others.

Q: And you think by Softening my Glare, the contamination and pollution of city life, the poverty, crime, and corruption will disappear?

A: No, it won't, but the tension within you will. Avoiding the calcification of your spirit, the accumulation of tension, or the onset of illness will enable you to empathise with others and help facilitate real change. We all have to start here and now with what we have and where we are.

Ensuring your own well-being ensures your ability to actively fight in other arenas too. Conversely, if you believe that only once the contamination and pollution of city life have been eradicated and that poverty, crime, and corruption have all been abolished, can we then attend to the needs of our own health, then you may have something of a wait.

Q: I'm still not convinced. My paws are registered with the local Veterinary Police Force, so I can carry real shurikens. In our school we are trained never to soften our glare, or our enemies will think we are an easy target.

A: What enemies? The 'E' numbers on a carton of milk? The exhaust fumes in the underground car park? The fatty deposits that are slowly hardening your arteries? You will only be an easy target if you live unconsciously and unhealthily. It's your choice.

Q: This is just verbal Bean Curd Boxing. If I had to practice Push Hands I would go for the jugular of my opponent.

A: In Push Hands, there is no opponent.

Q: Yes, OK. I get the Kwai Chang Caine bit—one-handed claps and all that stuff. But what if I really did go for the jugular?

A: Ok. In the act of 'going' you expose your intentions by telegraphing anticipation and muscular tension (particularly noticeable in city dwellers). In short, your intention signals to those who have learned to read the signs. If your Push Hands partner understands this language, they will relax and move their jugular out of the way. Or, if they wish to lose—and thereby win—they might expose their throat even more.

Q: Other than Frown Busting, Throat Exposing, and identifying 'E' numbers on supermarket shelves, what use is Bean Curd Boxing?

A: You mean other than learning to live more consciously, more contentedly, with better posture, better overall health, deeper breathing, greater fluidity, and employing all the wonderful ideas from the cookbooks of history: from Fish Frying to Dust Merging?

Q: Exactly. I don't need a bowl of Gazpacho. I need organised teaching. I need a class.

LOOKING BACK TO WALK FORWARD:

A BEAN CURD BOXER'S GUIDE TO TAI CHI HISTORY

Applied Tai Chi is learning to side-step your Aunt's political opinions at family dinners.

I t does not matter what Tai Chi Form you practice or what name it has been given; it only matters that you practice it. Learning only from a book has limitations, primarily because there is no one to correct your mistakes other than yourself. Learning in a local class or online is the obvious solution, but classes vary considerably from style to style and from teacher to teacher. So what criteria can you use when considering a class? Where do you go from this point to develop your Bean Curd Boxing? In this chapter, we are going to look at the roots of Tai Chi, specifically a Smattering of History, a Good Portion of Legend, and a Large Serving of Scepticism. Once equipped with such history, you will have a clearer idea of what Tai Chi is, what it can offer, and help you decide what you are really looking for.

ORANGUTANS, ORIGINS, AND OBJECTIVITY

The origins of Tai Chi are far from clear. One problem is that historical records, by nature, are subjective. This has never been truer than in the history of martial arts, where life and legend, fact and fiction are recited in one and the same breath. For some, this storytelling is a weakness; for others, it is a strength. If we can say anything with certainty, it is that everything we have is unquestionably uncertain. So, what point would there be in attempting such a controversial narrative? Well, if we browse the shelves of history, leaving in place all those books that claim authenticity and taking down only those that promise a little bit of context and background, we find ourselves with a blend of documentation and description that will help us visualise the routes this art has taken and the roots it has left behind.

A SMATTERING OF HISTORY

In those distant days before the invention of the printing press, skills and knowledge were handed down by word of mouth and by apprenticing oneself to a known master of the arts. This relationship was all-important and has fuelled the popular folklore and history of all the different martial arts. Information was transmitted slowly, selectively, and carefully to avoid knowledge and skills being spread outside the confines of a small, trusted group, family, or school. This was how the different families—Yang, Chen, Sun, and Wu—maintained their lineage and styles.

However, with the appearance of the printing press, this knowledge spread to a far greater number of people through the publication of manuals and instructional books. Today, the internet has further democratised this process by offering a space for knowledge and resources to be shared, ideas and approaches to be discussed, and a collective knowledge base to be built for a global community. Consequently, the need to hunt down a particular master who exclusively holds "secrets" or to apprentice oneself to a guru has become less important.

Styles too have adapted over time, and new ones have evolved from earlier versions, such as Wu Dang and Cheng (as in Cheng Man-ch'ing), or the Simplified Tai Chi style introduced by the Chinese Republic in 1956.

Being aware of the changing history enables us to look critically at a history that is notoriously unreliable, anecdotal, and heavily biased. We know little for certain, other than that the Tai Chi form was originally taught as a series of separate postures, and slowly developed into a unified movement just a few hundred years ago. Taught largely within the confines of the Chen family, Tai Chi only spread further when students from outside the family—Yang Lu Chan and Wu Yu-Hsing—popularised the art, turning it into something akin to what we see today.

THE IMPORTANCE OF LEGEND

In the absence of accurate historical data, history has borrowed heavily from legend, and in so doing, legend has come to assume the main stage in Tai Chi's controversial story. The legendary founder of the art, a man called Chang San Feng (of whom a word or two has been mentioned before), was said to have studied the movements of a crane fighting a serpent to develop the individual postures that would later become the Tai Chi Form. It is an inspiring and pictorial image, but unfortunately almost identical to the history of almost all other Chinese martial arts, each claiming to have been invented by an ancient sage who meticulously studied the movements of animals in combat.

Despite such implausibility, every art needs a Chang San Feng. For myth and legend convey the spirit in a way that recorded history often fails to do. The essence of any art is conveyed through stories that infuse history with not just facts, but with imagery, energy, charisma, and the obligatory tales of superhuman feats. Authenticated histories alone do little to excite or enthuse newcomers to any art. If the focus of history resides in fact, then, like Tai Chi, such accounts convey only controversy, bitterness, and thinly veiled subjectivity.

When we read the life story of Chang San Feng, we leave behind the mortal world of petty squabbles to be transported to the woodlands of ancient China. There, accompanied by his pet orangutan, the sage would walk for thousands of miles amongst the bamboo forests and green mountains, mumbling to the 10,000 things, observing animals in conflict, and practising his newly created postures. It is even said he taught a simian version to his fellow traveller. One assumes he also found time to teach non-simians en route, for if not, today we would only have very hairy teachers with extremely long arms.

Chang San Feng, it is said, lived for over 200 years and was last spotted in the Shantung province flying away on the back of a crane. His companion was not with him. In 1459, the Emperor of China declared him a Saint.

A LARGE SERVING OF SCEPTICISM

Historically, styles have taken their names from the families that have passed down the training from one generation to the next, even though each teacher in turn will have added or subtracted parts as they thought best. This has certainly been the history of the Yang style. It was Yang Lu Chan's popular modifications of the Chen Style, passed on to his grandson—Yang Chen Fu—that took the emphasis away from the martial aspect during the early part of the 20th century. Finally, one of his students, Cheng Man Ching, adapted the style even further, spreading Tai Chi across continents and cultures. The Chinese Government itself, in the 1950s, played a role in adapting the Yang Style for a wider audience by creating the new Combined Style.

The history of Tai Chi is a history of adaptation, and that is as it should be for an art built around the concept of change and usefulness. When we look at the different schools today, we are really looking at the history of different teachers, different teaching methods, and different audiences. Even though two classes can share the same name and the teachers taught by the same instructor, they may have a totally different approach to learning and practising Tai Chi.

So how can you tell if the school you are visiting is any good? The truth is that it may well depend on what you mean by good. For if you are looking for one thing out of Tai Chi—e.g., meditation— then the school that is emphasising the martial applications may not be the one for you, and vice-versa. It is worth remembering that despite the aura that you may detect around a teacher, a school, or the reputation that precedes either, perfection rarely exists in the human form, and all methods and practices have their good and bad points. This will probably come to light over the months that you attend the school. When you do find a few imperfections, don't worry, for it is often these that make the school and the teacher interesting.

One good starting point is to ask yourself: how best do you learn new things? Do you learn best by doing, by talking about, or by understanding?

CLASSES FOR THE STUDENT WHO LIKES DOING THINGS

There are no shortages of classes for doers. You will need to look for the traditional exponent of Tai Chi who prefers to show rather than tell. These teachers are the performers, the demonstrators, and they teach by example. They exhibit well, compete enthusiastically, and convey their lessons by encouraging imitation. Dialogue is minimal, except for related anecdotes, so explanations and contexts will need to be prised out of them with the edge of a Tai Chi sword. If you are the sort of student who is confident with your physical learning skills, observant, have a good eye for detail, and learn best by following and copying, then this is the category of class you should be looking for. The emphasis may well be on the martial side of Tai Chi, so look for the obvious clues: the presence of sparring mittens, weapons, and punch bags, and the absence of incense, candles, and tie-dyed clothing.

CLASSES FOR THE STUDENT WHO LIKES TALKING

If you like to verbally weigh up the pros and cons of life before engaging, then this will be the class for you. Look for a class with a teacher who has a good grasp of the general principles of Tai Chi and has received his or her training from one of the major schools. He or she will have attended a lot of seminars, weekend retreats, and completed many different courses. You may even see some certificates hanging on the wall and a few signed books strategically placed on a public mantelpiece. A photo or two may be hanging prominently above an incense-burning shrine, displaying a more youthful version of themselves alongside an older man with a wispy beard and crinkly eyes. These teachers articulate well the concepts behind the moves and often contextualise the lessons. Be careful, though, with those who have succumbed to the temptation to merge Tai Chi with other disciplines—Pilates-Chi, Jasmine-Tea, or Yoga-Tai—and who consequently either enrich or dilute the spirit of the style, according to your point of view. For visual clues when entering for the first time, look out for uniforms and badges, printed syllabuses, and the Tai Chi shopping catalogue subtly left open in the lobby to the school.

CLASSES FOR THE STUDENT WHO LIKES UNDERSTANDING THINGS

These classes are more difficult to find, and possibly with good reason. These teachers do not simply copy what has been done before but look at what they have learned and inherited and rework that according to the area, time, and people they are teaching. Like classes in Water Boiler Maintenance, Tai Chi can be complicated to learn and often demands more from a teacher than the ability to do or explain. The transmission of skills and knowledge to others requires inspiration, and this is a very difficult quality to find. This class of instructors does not fit neatly into any of the above categories. They probably will not follow any of the written guidelines regarding what you should or shouldn't do. They may not even teach many students, but find one of them and they will inspire the socks off you.

CUTTING THROUGH THE CURD

Like the circle of Yin and Yang, in the end, you will have to start at the beginning. Look to yourself, recognising what motivates you to learn and in what context. Do not despair if you cannot find all you seek from one teacher or from just one style. Some of the best practitioners have studied under more than one teacher, and in time—you too may follow that path. Be open, be flexible, and above all, be inspired.

ASK THE TEAPOT:

Q: If I were attending a class, why would I also need to practice at home?

A: Partly because daily practice helps to internalise the movements, and partly because the techniques only have application when they migrate out of the classroom. Tai Chi is a language, and like any new language, if you only study for one hour a week in the classroom, it is going to take an awful long time before you reach fluency.

Q: Do I need a shuriken belt and a Ninja Mask to learn Bean Curd Boxing?

A: Unlike many sports, Tai Chi requires no expensive training shoes, no breathable, tight, multi-coloured vests, nor safety hats or glasses. You do not even need a gym or a dojo to practice the techniques. Bean Curd Boxing should be practised while walking the streets, riding the underground, or standing in a queue. The lessons should be practised in discussions as you learn to parry an argument, defuse a debate, or yield to a point of view. These are the activities that need to be fused with your daily life. And none require an assassin's mask.

Q: Can't I just practice Bean Curd Boxing in my bedroom?

A: If you have the opportunity to practice in the fresh air, and somewhere public such as a park, then take the opportunity to do so! This is particularly true if you are learning the Form. At the beginning your practice will degenerate into a shivering external display, but over time you will accustom yourself to the presence of others, and you will learn to focus once more on your technique and internal state. This, in turn, will become a useful skill when performing during class activities or when learning to record your movements on your mobile phone in order to share with others for feedback. Being open to public scrutiny, positive criticism, and peer group encouragement are useful skills that spill over into all aspects of Bean Curd Boxing.

Q: Your advice on finding a class is useful, but how will I remember all this?

A: You don't need to. Simply take time out to watch a class, rather than just doing a trial session. Observe how the teacher interacts, participates, encourages, and see if they are ever silent, facilitating, or empowering.

Q: You still haven't told me what actually goes on in a Tai Chi class!

A: Apart from the Form and Pushing Hands, each class is different. Generally, you can expect a range of activities, from gentle limbering-up exercises to warm muscles to winding-down exercises to settle an overactive mind. Each week, a posture from the Form is learned with explanations of its origin, meaning, health benefits, or martial application. Some elements of the class are learned individually, others with partners, and others collectively.

Q: Would going to a Tai Chi class help my back pain, knee ache, insomnia, arthritis, toothache, bruised elbow (fill in as appropriate)?

A: Good question, and one that almost every student new to the art will ask at some point. Unfortunately, the answer depends on so many factors that it is impossible to give a simple yes/no answer. Much depends on your attitude, the severity of your condition, the amount of practice you put into learning, and how often you practice outside the class. Other important factors include your general constitution, immune system, blood circulation, and even your capacity for concentration. Talk to your instructor, talk to yourself, talk to your dog. In fact, talk to anyone who will listen, as it means you are engaging and assessing. These are excellent activities to maintain as you begin your practice and as you check on your progress. Many students do experience real improvements in health and balance very soon after starting. Try searching for Tai Chi health research on the web and you may surprise yourself. Just don't get distracted on YouTube.

Q: I'm interested in learning The Form. Can you just tell me in simple words how long it will take me to learn? And please, no metaphors or Kwai Chang Caine speak.

A: Only you can answer that. There are many deciding factors, including commitment, patience, and time. Learning the Form may also depend on how much you need to undo before you can begin to acquire.

Q: You mean buttons?

A: Let's just say layers.

Q: That's Kwai Chang Caine speak!

A: OK. Let's say it takes about the same time to walk around a circle.

Q: What size of circle?

A: Exactly. If you are lucky enough to find a good school with a motivating teacher, you will keep walking for the rest of your days. If you are unlucky and find a bad school, one of two things will happen:

1. The end of the circle will appear too distant, and you will give up, citing reasons of time, inability to memorise so many detailed moves, or a lack of binoculars.
2. You will complete the circle too quickly and find it a shallow experience, having only touched on the breathing/form/candle-meditation version or the deadly secret five-finger freestyle martial technique.

In either case, you need to find a more balanced class. Remember, Tai Chi has no grading system. Unlike the Japanese arts of Karate, Aikido, and Judo, there are no coloured belts, oral exams, or multiple-choice tests. This can lead to difficulties for Westerners as we are used to grading our learning with performance-related tests. Tai Chi, however, is circular, and it is not easy to mark someone's progress in a circle. A student's rate of progress depends on many factors: personal experience, regularity of prac-tice, and a commitment to throw it all away should it become a chore.

Remember what Lao Tzu said:

"Nature does not hurry; yet everything is accomplished."

Q: I'm a member of the Taoist Terrapins Temple, and I believe that your degenerative and flippant interpretations of the Tai Chi principles do little but harm the efforts of the Tai Chi community to work together in harmony.

A: "Harmony" is achieved through mutual respect for differences, not through enforced homogenisation, whether that derives from an ideology, a lineage, or simply a dominant position in the structure of organised martial arts.

Q: Taoist Terrapins participate in competitions whilst Bean Curd Boxers do not. You talk about applying your art, yet we are the only style that really converts words into action.

A: Bean Curd Boxers decide for themselves whether to participate in competitions. For us, "applied" does not merely mean martial; it means how useful this training is outside the classroom. There are many ways to test skills and understanding. One is to see how far we can reach out to others without losing our rootedness.

Q: How then is a student to know whether a Bean Curd Boxer or a Taoist Terrapin is right?

A: By the sort of questions that are asked.

Q: Well, ahm...in that case...ahh.

A: All students must decide for themselves what is right for them. However, they do not have to do it alone, for there is a set of guiding principles to help them make their decision. These principles are contained in what is elusively referred to as The Classics, a collection of writings spanning thousands of years that define the physical, mental, and spiritual path of development.

CHAPTER 13

IT'S ALL BEEN SAID BEFORE:

LESSONS IN FLOW, WISDOM, AND EMBRACING OPPOSITES

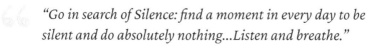

"Go in search of Silence: find a moment in every day to be silent and do absolutely nothing...Listen and breathe."

I n the practice of Tai Chi, it matters little what school or what master you learn from, whether you practice the 24, 36, or 725 posture versions, or whether your form is described as long, short, big, small, or enormous. These are all relative terms. What is far more important than any label is that you should try to follow the spirit, if not the literal word, of the Tai Chi Classics. The Classics are considered fundamental in understanding the principles of Tai Chi and Bean Curd Boxing. If possible, get hold of a copy of these texts yourself and look for the sections most appropriate to your practice.

After all, what appears magical to one person can be mundane to another. This does not mean you should selectively choose only some sections to follow and ignore the rest; rather, become familiar with the texts and find those that inspire your practice.

CHANG SAN FENG

We met Chang San Feng earlier in the book. He was a Taoist monk, a friend to orange-coloured simians, and the mythical creator of the individual Tai Chi postures. Some of the principles attributed to him include:

- In each movement, the whole body must be light and nimble. More important still, all movements must be continuous.
- In all movements, the inner strength is rooted in the feet, developed in the thighs, controlled by the waist, and expressed through the fingers. From the feet to the thighs, to the waist, and to the fingers, there must be complete co-ordination so that whether you are in advance or retreat, you will be in a favourable position.

- In any movement where there is up, there must be down; when there is front, there must be rear; and when there is left, there must be right. If one wishes to execute an upward movement, a downward one must precede it. This is like the idea of uprooting an object—the first thing you do is push it down.

In the words of Chang San Feng, we can see many of the principles we have covered in the Bean Curd Boxing Manual: softness and continuity of movement, finding your root and your centre, and the embracing of opposites. In the Tai Chi Form, each posture includes a little of its opposite—turning right before moving left, sinking before rising, etc. This is a direct application of Yin and Yang; everything always contains the seed of its opposite.

WANG CHUNG-YUEH

Wang Chung-Yueh was credited with combining the individual postures into one loose form. In a literal sense, it was Wang who combined the words into a sentence and thereby gave Tai Chi a fluid expression. Some of his written principles include:

- Tai Chi...is the mother of Yin and Yang. In motion, they separate; in stillness, they fuse.
- Keep your neck erect and direct the crown of your head upwards as if your neck were suspended from above...allow your intrinsic energy to sink to the tan tien, approximately three inches below your navel. (See Questions and Answers for more on Tan Tien) Avoid inclining your body in any direction.
- Reply to force on your left by emptying the left. Reply to force on your right by emptying the right. The more

someone pushes against you, the more they feel no resistance. The more they advance, the more you retreat. The more they retreat, the more you advance.

- Your body should be as light as a feather—a fly could not land on it without setting it in motion.
- Only when one can be extremely pliable and soft can one be extremely firm and hard.
- Bear in mind that when one part of the body moves, all other parts of the body move. When one part of the body comes to a standstill, all other parts do so too.

The literal interpretations of Wang Chung-Yueh's words continue to be debated by different scholars, but it is worth remembering that his words convey more than a simple set of instructions. When we try too hard to achieve something, the effort splits our energy into different directions. But when we  relax, our energy returns to the centre and fuses once more, just like when we start the Form and our energy begins to move away from our centre, shifting one way and then the next. At the final movement, everything comes to a quiet close again, and all separation disappears as we return to the same point from which we started.

YANG CHENG-FU

Yang Cheng-Fu was the grandson of Yang Lu Chan, the founder of the Yang Style of Tai Chi. Yang Lu Chan was the teacher of Tai Chi to the Imperial family and the Manchu Imperial Guards in the

Forbidden City. Yang Lu Chan became famous for never losing a battle nor harming his opponents, although details are vague as to exactly how this was achieved.

When Yang Cheng-Fu took over the teaching and development of Tai Chi from his grandfather, he did so against an extraordinarily interesting backdrop of Chinese history. During the final years of Manchu rule, from 1899 to 1901, the perceived invulnerability of Chinese culture and martial arts was challenged by an invasion of foreign armies that had entered the country to fight against the members of The Fists of Righteous Harmony, more popularly known as the 'Boxers'. The Boxers were those Chinese who felt that their way of life was under threat and were attempting to prevent the large-scale infiltration of Chinese society by Western culture and technology. The 'Boxer Rebellion', as it was termed in English, had innumerable consequences for Chinese culture and society, one of which was the realisation that the martial arts themselves were no match for the superior weaponry of the thousands of Western Alliance troops that had entered the country and violently put down the Boxer resistance.

Perhaps, by appreciating this context, we can understand why Yang Cheng-Fu began to shift the emphasis of the art away from its martial roots towards the needs of one's physical and mental well-being.

Some of Yang Cheng-Fu's principles include:

- The hands must follow the waist; do not move them independently.
- Drop your shoulders and sink your elbows.
- Apply your will and not your force.
- The end of one movement is the beginning of the next.

- Wear a hat and sunglasses when possible. (I may have mis-quoted this last one)

CHENG MAN-CH'ING

Cheng Man-ch'ing was a student of Yang Cheng-Fu, and many credit him with the widespread popu-larity of Tai Chi outside China, particularly in North America in the 1960s. Cheng Man-ch'ing was a controversial figure who left China—like many others after the revolution—to seek refuge overseas. His adaptation of the Yang Style—shortening the Form and adapting the postures—led to much criticism from many practitioners who believed that he had changed too much of the original style and argued that such fundamental changes consti-tuted a new style altogether. Despite the controversy, his version of the Tai Chi Yang Form remains popular and widely practiced all over the world and appears to have achieved a special resonance among Western audiences. Cheng Man-ch'ing was not only a profound practitioner of Tai Chi but also a 'Master of the Five Excellencies': Chinese medicine, Tai Chi Chuan, calligraphy, paint-ing, and poetry.

Some of his principles include:

- In brush knee, single whip, step and punch, etc., the knee must not extend beyond the foot, and the instep should be as soft as cotton.
- At the end of each movement, there must be a swing, and before the end of each swing, a new movement begins.

Round and round without end...uninterrupted continuity.

Here, Cheng Man-ch'ing is referring to the idea of Finding the Curve. In his version of the Form, all movements are circular. This allows for smoother transitions and a continuous flow of energy throughout. It also helps in using the natural momentum of each posture as we shift our weight and slide through one move after another.

ASK THE TEAPOT:

Q: When Wang Chung-Yueh said that a fly cannot land without setting the body in motion, was he referring to his poor swatting skills?

A: A good question that must ultimately be answered by everyone's inner fly-swat. I believe Wang was referring once more to the unity of our body and mind. Just like touching the surface of a still pond or body of water with your finger, ripples form and move out across the surface as the water adapts and yields to the force; so too the body.

Q: Chang San Feng said that in order to shift up, one must first head down, if left then right and if forwards then first backwards. Is this the spiral speech of the arboreal animals?

A: Chang San Feng is cleverly referring to the idea of embracing opposites and playing in the world of contradictions. For example, for us to walk forward, our feet have to push back against the ground. In order to turn left, we first need to push right. These are just simple laws of physics and have little to do with the chattering of chimps.

Q: What is this 'Tan Tien' and where can I download one?

A: The Tan Tien, according to Traditional Chinese Medicine, is an energy centre in the body that is referred to as a point of attention for energy breathing exercises and, because of its physical location, a focus for balance exercises. However, controversy surrounds the exact location of this point. Some claim it to be three, four, or nine centimetres below the navel, while others swear to have spotted it between the kidneys and the navel. We can probably only say with confidence that it is somewhere in the general region of the belly. An artist or warrior could be said to be moving from their Tan Tien if acting in accordance with their energy and spirit.

Q: If a Bean Curd Boxer were to summarise the main practices during each day, using less esoteric descriptions than you find in the world of Tai Chi, what would they be?

A: Well, as we started, so shall we finish. The form is circular, so too the advice:

1. Drink more water.
2. Breathe deeply and often.
3. Sleep well.
4. Practise regularly some form of exercise.
5. Go in search of Silence: find a moment in every day to be silent and do absolutely nothing. Turn off the mobile device. Close the laptop. Listen and breathe.
6. Keep your Bean Curd firm and enjoy your practice.

GETTING OUT OF YOUR OWN WAY:

STEP OUT, STEP BACK, AND WATCH THE WORLD UNFOLD

Wen looking to change anything or everything in life, learn to get out of your own way. Learn to let go of the memory of muscles, the chatter of a cheetah, or the temptation to prod that fish a little longer.

Change happens. Things do get done. The Universe moves on. We simply need to stop trying so hard.

When we stop trying so hard, our breath and energy no longer fragment: we maintain our rootedness and stay grounded. In this simple state of relaxation, we allow our uncarved—or natural—state to come through.

Relax, and we let the 10,000 Things come together, and suddenly ordinary moments become extraordinary: shapes emerge from the shadows of dust, and a procession of chimps, tortoises, flamingos, and ninjas all appear to come to our aid.

ASK THE TEAPOT

Q: I'm definitely interested in becoming a Bean Curd Boxer. What's the first step?

In the next section, you'll find a list of video examples to explore. But if you'd rather stay away from digital devices—and who can blame you—then simply follow your imagination.

Put aside this manual and step outside through the front door. Step out confidently with the Walk of a Cat, the directional sense of Chang San Feng, and the poise of a Damp Flamingo. Stroll out in search of Wind in which to Bathe, a Tiger to Embrace, or the Grumble of your Stomach to pursue. Stroll out to claim life as a series of free lessons in Bean Curd Boxing.

THE BEAN CURD PLAYGROUND

9 SMALL STEPS

A private Video playlist to discover examples and exercises to enrich your sense of Bean Curd play.

Welcome to the Bean Curd Playground—a private video playlist of exercises and insights. There's no need to sign up for a course or join anything. In fact, you don't even have to take a look at them if you'd rather not. You probably have more interesting things to do, like making a pot of tea or watching the sunset.

But for those curious to see examples of the exercises in the workshops, with a few added videos for your entertainment, just follow either of the links below.

My hope is that collectively, these videos will either deepen your sense of play or distract you from the 10,000 things you should be doing. Either way, they will have served their purpose.

To access the Bean Curd Playground, simply use any digital device with a camera. Point it at the QR code below, and you'll be transported to the Bean Curd Playlist. No camera? No problem! Just follow the URL below.

https://youtube.com/playlist?list=PLBt5EL-f6QfTA8Qr7PIU7W GUNhHlbhKzE&si=3b7nWZc_1T8y8QYF

WORKSHOP 1: SWING AND MOMEMNTUM

The Chimp: Let your movements flow with natural instinct—never rigid, always ready to shift, climb, and swing to new heights. Fist-bump fate, eat fruit with abandon, and never take things too seriously. Remember: a well-thrown banana can solve most things.

Video 1 in the Bean Curd Playground list is all about swinging. But if you don't have any playful chimps to lend a hairy hand, you can still explore the movements by trying out the simple waist exercises in this video: Swing and Momentum (do watch out for banana skins).

WORKSHOP 2: LYING DOWN & BREATHING

The Earth: Embrace Gaia in Video 2, where you'll explore the first stage of Abdominal Breathing and grounding yourself. It doesn't get much easier than simply lying down and feeling your breath move. Lay flat, breathe deeply into your belly, and let gravity do the work. Feel yourself sink into the floor, grounding yourself as you watch your abdomen rise with each breath.

WORKSHOP 3: SEATED BREATHING

The Mountain: Sit tall, breathe deeply into your belly, and feel the earth beneath your feet.

With each breath, grow more rooted, more steady, more unshakable. Video 3 builds on the previous exercise, continuing the focus on breathing, but this time, sitting upright like a mountain as you observe the rise and fall of your abdomen.

WORKSHOP 4: FEET BREATHING & POSTURE

The Tree: Breathe through your feet and feel your roots sinking deep into the earth. Draw energy from the ground, let it rise, and stand connected to the world. Video 4 introduces you to the basics of good posture, combined with mindful breathing and grounding, so you can apply these principles as you move through your daily activities.

WORKSHOP 5: SHAKE IT OUT

The Dancing Orangutan: Video 5 introduces you to a gentle shaking exercise, inspired by those solitary arboreal forest people with long, hairy arms. For when you swing through the trees, there is no rush; instead, move with quiet wisdom. Calculate, adapt, and flow effortlessly from branch to green-leafed branch. Let your movements be deliberate yet fluid, experiencing the cool air in your fur and the sensation of qi energy moving through your body.

WORKSHOP 6: BAMBOO IN THE WIND

The Bamboo: Bend with the wind, grow in unexpected places, and remain rooted yet flexible. Life's storms pass, but the suppleness of the bamboo endures. Video 6 teaches you how to develop good posture and a sense of grounding as you learn to stand up for the things that matter to you.

WORKSHOP 7: CAT WALKING

The Cat: When you encounter a challenge, don't resist it—weave around it, slip through it, or leap over it, but always land on your feet. Stalk the mysteries of the universe, nap in dusty sunbeams, and chase invisible mice. Remember, the world is your scratching post. Video 7 shows you how, not only to stalk, but to walk like a cat.

WORKSHOP 8: STAND LIKE A FLAMINGO

The Flamingo: Video 8 focuses on improving your balance by letting go of rigidity. Let your movements be as fluid as a flamingo's dance, yet as steady as its stance. Don't let anyone tell you that you can't share their puddle. Learn to sip wisdom from the edge of all puddles, and remember: where the winds shift and the waters stir, it is there you will find your poise and balance.

WORKSHOP 9: DRIVE LIKE A TORTOISE

The Tortoise: Video 9 concludes by reminding you of the benefits of slow, steady, and deliberate movements. Take your time with both the important and mundane aspects of life. Learn to crawl through this labyrinth into which you are born, with your house on your back and eternity in your gaze. Remember: in stillness, there is strength; in patience, there is power.

About the Teapotmonk

Just to be clear, Paul Read is neither a teapot nor a monk.

He was born restless in the very centre of London, England, and now fidgets his way back and forth between the UK and Spain in search of good coffee, good conversation, and fresh vegetables.

In the absence of finding these, he spends his time writing and designing freshly brewed and 100% guru-free, online courses that promote a more collaborative, flexible, and less dogmatic approach to learning Tai Chi.

Book Store

taichi-store.com

Training Site

21stcenturytaichi.com

Articles and information

teapotmonk.com

Acknowledgments

This book would never have been completed were it not for the following:

INSPIRATION:

- My first Karate teacher, who taught me that smaller could be better and that softness could overcome anything.
- My first Gung-Fu teacher, who showed me that rhythm plays as vital a part in the martial arts as any technique.
- My first Tai Chi teacher, who demonstrated that language expresses itself in our very being, as well as in our chosen words.

- My father, who taught me that laughter enables distance and clarity, that adaptability and change are to be forever embraced.

ASSISTANCE:

My old friend Ian Betts for his speedy revisions, advice, and words of encouragement for the 1st edition.

My 'media-naranja' Cherry[1] for offering creative insights when mine had all but expired, and for help shaping a book that would endure the passing of time.

PERSISTENCE:

For Sophie and her refusal to heed medical advice, and Mr. Y. Bear, who taught me to see and hear another world I had overlooked.

IMAGES

Since the first release of the Manual in 2010, the images that appear in the book have undergone constant change, being updated with each new edition. Digital art programs have evolved at lightening speed, enhanced further by recent new movements in text to image prompting. For the 5th edition of this book, this new collaborative method arose that gave rise to a new set of images, which were finally completed within traditional digital art programs. It was a curious journey, and one that I am sure, we are only just embarking upon.

---

1. https://creativecoaching.cherryjeffs.com/

WORDS

The ideas were first typed out in Word, back in 2010 and they largely remain untouched. More recent editions have updated titles, newly added Q&A sections, and, slowly, I have hunted down and removed the elusive typos. Fortunately, digital writing tools have improved immensely since the era of Word, so all my research today, edits and all changes are carried out in an excellent writing tool called Scrivener, then exported to be formatted in Vellum before being sent to the printer.

SPELLING

It is argued that the older spellings for the arts of **Tai Chi** and **Chi Gong** (Wade-Giles transliterations) are both redundant and anachronistic and should now be replaced by **Taiji** and **Qigong** (Pinyin transliterations) introduced by the Chinese government in 1958.

This is generally true, however, despite Government proclamations, popular culture works to its own rhythm and consequently the use of **Tai Chi** stubbornly refuses to die in the West, much to the despair and horror of many in the field. **Qigong**, however, has now established itself over the rapidly diminishing **Chi Gong**.

Somewhat confusingly, you will find in these pages both **Tai Chi** and **Qigong**. I use simply what is in common usage, in the same way I continue to write Lao Tzu over Lǎozi, Chang San-feng over Zhāng Sānfēng, or Taoism over Daoism. This may change by the time the next edition is released, as such, echoes the ebb and flow of common usage changes our linguistic and written practices.

REFERENCES

Below you will find sources on the health articles I have referenced in the book, as well as other links to practices and writings on Tai Chi, including a list of books I have referred to in specific chapters.

ARTICLE: WALKING DOWN STAIRS

The benefits of walking down stairs (exercising eccentrically[1]) are often overlooked by our preference to go up whenever possible. Yet, in true Yin fashion, many benefits are to be had by seeking the bottom of the valley or lower floor, including:

- Improved muscle strength
- Enhanced bone density
- Better balance and coordination
- Cardiovascular health
- Caloric burn and metabolic benefits

Walking down stairs engages the quadriceps and promotes eccentric muscle contractions, which can lead to greater muscle strength, and stimulates bone growth.

Studies show that individuals who regularly walk down stairs can experience significant improvements in muscle function and strength, with one study[2] noting a 34% increase in muscle

---

1.   http://www.teapotmonk.com/tai-chi-articles/tai-chi-fitness-and-eccentric-exercises
2.   https://theindependent.sg/the-strange-reason-why-walking-down-the-stairs-is-better-than-walking-up-for-your-body/

strength for those descending stairs compared to those ascending. Other studies[3] seem to verify these findings.

So next time you see an escalator in front of you, ride it with a guilt-free conscience. Just remember, walk down.

THE BENEFITS OF STANDING LIKE A FLAMINGO

As reported by both the Guardian newspaper[4] and the BBC[5], a study published in the British Journal of Sports Medicine found that middle-aged and elderly people who cannot balance on one leg for 10 seconds are almost twice as likely to die within 10 years compared to those who can.

It appears that no follow up reports have been conducted showing those found to be spending inordinate amounts of time standing on one leg, later fell over and were run over by a bus or an escaped rhino.

In the absence of such contradictory reports, we must therefore conclude that there is a direct correlation between balance ability and mortality risk.

3. https://cathe.com/walking-upstairs-burns-more-calories-but-walking-down stairs-is-healthy-too-heres-why/
4. https://www.theguardian.com/society/2022/jun/20/balancing-on-one-leg-useful-health-test-later-life-research
5. https://www.bbc.co.uk/programmes/articles/35QytBYmkXJ4JnDYl9zYngb/ why-you-should-stand-on-one-leg

DRIVE LIKE A TORTOISE: GO SLOW

Research on traffic speeds in urban situations: "Smoothing Urban Traffic Flow with Lighter Vehicle Masses and Smarter Driving Behaviours". 2011 University of West England and Toyota Manufacturing UK

OTHER ARTICLES REFERRED TO @ TEAPOTMONK.COM

- Alan Watts life and meaning[6]
- The importance of circles
- Eccentric Exercising[7]
- Best Tai Chi Books[8]

BOOKS

- Embrace Tiger Return to Mountain by Al Chung-Liang
- The Watercourse Way by Alan Watts.
- Tai Chi Illustrated Workbook by Paul Read
- One Last Thing by Paul Read
- The Tao of Jeet Kune Do by Bruce Lee.
- The Tao of Pooh by Benjamin Hoff
- The Tao Te Ching - Versions by Ron Hogan, William Martin and Ursula Le Guin would be my choices.
- The Way of the Hound by Mr. Y. Bear and Paul Read
- There are no Secrets by Wolf Lowenthal

---

6.   https://www.teapotmonk.com/alan-watts-his-life-and-philosophy

7.   https://www.teapotmonk.com/tai-chi-articles/tai-chi-fitness-and-eccentric-exercises

8.   https://www.teapotmonk.com/best-books-on-taichi

ND - #0172 - 020125 - C33 - 210/148/11 - PB - 9781836029069 - Matt Lamination